Marketing Automation Untang

**How My Journey Can Improve
Your Marketing Operations Game**

Author: Diederik Martens

Marketing Automation

"A practice by marketers to plan, manage, coordinate, test, improve, and measure their marketing efforts, both online and offline, through technology, processes, data, and best practices. To also streamline marketing and sales and closely manage and nurture generated leads, aiming to convert leads into customers. To also upsell, cross sell, and retain customers. And to inform, engage, and satisfy customers and create brand ambassadors."

Diederik Martens

Title: Marketing Automation Untangled
Subtitle: How My Journey Can Improve Your Marketing Operations Game

Author: Diederik Martens
Published by: Amazon

Diederik Martens is the CEO & Founder / Chief Marketing Technologist at Chapman Bright.

First Edition: January 2022
Second Edition: April 2022

ISBN: 9798799635695

A SPECIAL THANK YOU TO

My wife Silvy and my daughters Suze and Iza
for letting me write quite a few chapters during our holiday in France
during the summer of 2020 and during a solitary retreat in April 2021. I
hope that when they read this book,
they and many of my friends and family
better comprehend what I do for a living.
Especially after reading Appendix I. ;-)

My Chapman Bright colleagues Jacques and Katja
for reviewing some of the first chapters in the summer of 2020
and for providing me with great feedback to continue writing.

Scott Brinker and Frank Geldof
for proofreading and providing testimonials prior to release.

Warren Knight
for inspiring me to dust off my idea for writing this book.

My former colleagues at Quintiq
for believing in my ideas and for allowing me to experiment and grow.

Everybody that contributed on LinkedIn
By responding to my LinkedIn question in late November 2019
on what should be included in this book.
In particular, the following contributors:
Souhaib Aouini, Muhammad Ardhin, Henrik Becker,
Stefan Callebaut, Jeff Coveney, Pieter van Dijken, Melanie Gipp, Eoin
Johnson, Katja Keesom, Jeff Kew, Anne-Marie Kleiss,
Elliott Lowe, Janine Olariu, Jan-Henrik Reimann, Arthur Roche, Thomas
Tack, Rob Tersteeg, and Jan Peter Verheuvel

Marketing Automation
Untangled.com

"Diederik is one of the pioneering practitioners of marketing technology and operations management. In this engaging book, he takes you on his journey in the field and delivers a terrific guide to real-world success with marketing automation. Highly recommend."

Scott Brinker
Editor, chiefmartec.com / Author, *Hacking Marketing*

"Diederik's journey is an interesting insight on how to roll into Marketing Automation and how to be great at it. It not only confirms that I am on the right track but also has given me new ideas on how to improve myself."

Frank Geldof
Marketing Automation Platform Manager at Ericsson

"Few experts are able to convey the benefits that complex technology can bring to a client organisation audience convincingly and understandably. Diederik has the rare combination of deep technical subject matter and technology adaptation expertise that was fundamental to the success of the marketing automation implementation that I was fortunate to be a part of. His knowledge and approach on how to implement marketing automation shared in this book is extremely valuable to anyone in the consideration or implementation phase of such project."

Pieter van Ouwerkerk
Marketing Director at DHL Express, The Netherlands

"Diederik has gifted us with a juicy guide from the trenches with lots of useful practical insights for anyone embracing this path. On top of that, he also brings an inspiring journey on how to transform our skills into a successful consulting business."

Rui Rodrigues
CIO & Global Digital Business Director at BIAL

PREFACE

Stockholm, Sweden, Nov. 25, 2019 — I am providing a keynote speech at Marketing Automation Day in Sweden tomorrow. It's a spinoff on a keynote I have presented before. I share my journey to achieving successful marketing automation to help the audience untangle marketing automation themselves, so they too can become successful.

Mikael from Wednesday Relations picks me and another speaker up from the airport. The other speaker, Warren Knight, immediately makes an impression on me, and we decide to continue our discussion during dinner at the hotel of the event. Warren shares his story about how he was an agency owner and how he became an author and professional speaker. And I share my journey in MarTech. I tell Warren that I've been thinking about writing about my marketing automation experience for several years now, but I simply did not have the time. Especially not now with Chapman Bright, my MarTech agency, entering the scale-up phase. Later that night, I go to bed, but my brain remains hyperactive. I can't sleep! I keep thinking about putting my marketing automation experiences on paper. Presenting my marketing automation experience helps others, but writing a book about it will allow me to share many more details. It could help even more marketing leaders and marketing technologists avoid pitfalls in marketing automation and become successful.

It's morning, still dark in Sweden, and I grab a coffee. Then I head out to the first floor, where they wire me up with a microphone. I watch Warren's keynote. As he leaves the stage, I'm announced. I finish my keynote about my years at Quintiq. With less than three hours on the clock before I will moderate an open-space table, we decide to have lunch together with a friend of Warren's, who also frequently works as a speaker. Adam Strong is so kind to also briefly show us the city center.

I can't stop thinking about this book . . .

During dinner later that day, I make up my mind on the structure of the book. It should read like a business novel, like a story, almost like a biography. Mostly chronologically. Sometimes with flashbacks to earlier periods. It will have stories and context for all the lessons I've learned and all the pitfalls, tips, tricks, and cases I've come across in more than a decade of working in marketing automation. And where possible, I'll switch to theory and inject all the relevant methods, models, and templates I've come up with throughout the years. And then it will switch back to the storyline. In the first chapters, I'll share my first methods and solutions, while in later chapters, I'll share the more refined versions. I want you, the reader, to keep getting better at marketing automation with every chapter you read, just like I did.

Back in my hotel room, I open my LinkedIn app on my iPhone and ask my followers what they would like me to write. I received many responses, and I'd like to thank all the contributors for all their inspiration!

The next morning, I check into a business lounge at Arlanda airport and open up my notebook. I write down the first key milestones that come to mind. These will become the chapters for the book. Why not start writing right here and now? The result? This preface, written at Arlanda Airport on November 27, 2019. Finished and reviewed minutes before boarding my plane back to Amsterdam.

Now I'd like to take you on a journey to successful marketing automation. A journey that had already started during my studies around the year 2000. But first, let me take you back to December 2012, when for the first time in my career, marketing automation became part of my job title when I started at a software company called Quintiq.

TABLE OF CONTENTS

Marketing Automation Untangled

**How My Journey Can Improve
Your Marketing Operations Game**

MY FIRST MARKETING AUTOMATION JOB

It's 2012, and I'm monitoring job sites for a client-side marketing automation position in the Netherlands. The Netherlands and the United Kingdom are both front-runners in this field in Europe. There must be a client-side position somewhere? Unfortunately, there are only a handful of agency-side positions. But I want to get out of the agency I am working for right now. In late 2012, I finally find the dream job I'm looking for. A software company is looking for a marketing automation specialist. It's Quintiq, a company I had never heard of, but it's just a twenty-five-minute drive from my home.

Quintiq is a software company in the supply chain planning and optimization space. They won the fastest-growing company award multiple times, and I'm employee #611 to join the company. Quintiq will play a significant role in the development of my marketing automation skills and experience. That's why I think it's important to provide you with a bit more context on their business.

Quintiq has more than fifteen offices on four continents and employs some of the brightest in the country (e.g., chess champions). The company was founded in the Netherlands by five consultants. One of them was a math teacher. Quintiq's solutions can optimize any process in workforce, logistics, and/or production. But that is not something clients want to hear. Clients think their process is unique, and they want to hear that the product can solve their exact challenge. So that's the first marketing challenge.

> *"Clients think their process is unique, and they want to hear the product can solve their exact challenge."*

Quintiq has a matrix organization, a few horizontal departments (such as finance, legal, IT, marketing, quality management, etc.), and twelve vertical business units. Each unit is managed by two or three directors: a commercial director, a technical director, and sometimes a delivery director. Four regional vice-presidents are each responsible for three business units. Business units can focus on a region or an industry vertical.

13

My first day is at the global headquarters in Den Bosch, the Netherlands. I'm part of the global marketing team, which is headed by the marketing director, who reports to the chief operations officer. The global marketing department has several teams: the content team that I'm part of, the sales operations team that is headed by Rob Tersteeg, someone for public relations, and an in-house agency (the OMT) located at our global development center in Kuala Lumpur, Malaysia.

The team in Kuala Lumpur has analytics experts, search engine advertising and search engine optimization experts, developers, writers, editors, and designers on the team. They created an in-house platform called MIRA, which stands for Marketing Innovation Request Avenue. It has many project management capabilities, mostly targeted at the creation of content (e.g., whitepapers).

Quintiq uses Salesforce Sales Cloud as their primary customer relations management (CRM). Rob, manager of the sales operations team, is responsible for Salesforce. Marketo Engage is the marketing automation platform (MAP) they implemented a few months before I joined. Quintiq is leveraging the native integration between Marketo Engage and Salesforce to exchange data between both platforms. Quintiq uses more marketing technology than just Marketo Engage and Salesforce, but I'm sharing these two with you first. Why? I believe your CRM and MAP are much like the left and right chambers of the heart for your marketing and sales operations. They are essential for making the other organs work.

> *"Your CRM and MAP are much like the left and right chambers of the heart for your marketing and sales operations."*

In the first few weeks, I'm getting acquainted with the platforms, the team, and the product. In my third week, however, things suddenly change. Quintiq leadership announces that, in alignment with the American investors, they finally hired an American chief marketing officer (CMO), who will be stationed at our Philadelphia headquarters. He replaces the Netherlands-based marketing director. Jeff Vail quickly announces that he won't be making any organizational changes in the short term.

In the first weeks of 2013, I continue diving into Marketo Engage and Salesforce. I noticed that the platforms are mostly used for sending simple mail blasts. And there are some elementary scoring workflows. And every lead, regardless of its score, is synced directly to a queue in Salesforce, which acts like a waitlist. A team of inside sales representatives manually distribute leads from these queues to sales colleagues around the world. There is no automation. And it usually takes up to seventy-two hours to get a lead to the right colleague. Sometimes a lead goes to the wrong colleague, which results in the lead cooling down even more. I quickly realize what Quintiq's highest priority is.

Scoring in marketing automation means assigning points to properties and behaviors that imply a propensity to buy. Leads with higher scores should have a higher propensity to buy. Nurturing is engaging with a lead (e.g., through emails) until they are ready to buy.

"Best-in-class companies have up to eight times more deals per 1,000 inquiries."
SiriusDecisions

I defined three short-term projects. First, implement a basic lead management process to track and assign success. Second, automate the lead assignment to reduce time to contact. Third, make sure there's some basic nurturing to distinguish between hot and cold leads. This way, sales can focus on those with a greater propensity to buy.

Basic Lead Management to Manage Success

In 2013, most people were very proud if they could tie some revenue attribution to their marketing efforts. This was typically done through their business intelligence platform (BI) and typically only seen at a high level. However, I think you should be able to attribute very specific marketing efforts by an individual directly to specific deals. This will allow marketing leaders to better allocate budgets, and it will allow them to make data-driven decisions. Most companies want this but struggle with pulling it off. They can't seem to connect their deals to their marketing efforts. And that's exactly why they fail.

Stop trying to connect an effect to a cause after the fact. Instead, you should start at the beginning. Implement the processes required from the start so you don't have to connect it at the end. It all starts with a lead management process. If you don't have one, you should be worried. I mean very worried!

"If you don't have a proper lead management process in place, you should be very worried!"

I don't want to invent the wheel myself. And I want to make sure people adopt the new process. That's why I'm choosing a famous model. The SiriusDecisions Waterfall. There's a fair chance you know this process, but you might not have realized who invented it. Does the abbreviation *MQL* ring a bell?

Inquiry > Marketing Qualified Lead (MQL) > Sales Accepted Lead (SAL) > Sales Qualified Lead (SQL) > Deal

I set up a meeting with the marketing director, the new chief marketing officer (Jeff), and the head of sales operations (Rob). Four individuals means four opinions. The result? What the Dutch call a Polder Model. Not the ideal outcome, but a compromise in which everybody sees their most important elements. Though it's quite close to the Waterfall model. At this point, Quintiq has a strong sales-oriented culture. The new lead management process is an opportunity for marketing to bring more to the table. Marketing does generate quite a few new names for sales to follow up on, but up till now, every newly generated name goes directly to a queue in Salesforce.

Sales doesn't fully trust marketing to select which leads to push to Salesforce yet. The new lead management process changes all of that. Without too much attention, I make a soft cut in the process, which allows Marketo to control which leads go to Salesforce. Though without withholding any leads yet. At this point, I did not know that I would be reimplementing a full best-practice lead management process just eighteen months later. Here is the simple setup I started with:

1. Create the following fields in CRM and MAP:
   a. Life Cycle Stage (String)
   b. Life Cycle DateTime (Date-Time)

2. Create workflows in your MAP (or CRM) to stamp both fields:
   a. Stamp the system date-time in the Life Cycle DateTime field whenever the value changes for the Life Cycle Stage field.
   b. Anonymous lead becomes known: Stamp Life Cycle Stage with "Known".
   c. If the lead meets your marketing qualification criteria, then stamp the stage with "MQL". I'll get back to the possible criteria below.
   d. If the stage becomes "MQL", then assign it to a queue in your CRM instead of syncing every lead.
   e. When the owner changes from the queue to a user, stamp the stage with "SAL". When they take it out of the queue, you could say they accepted/assigned the lead.
   f. When an opportunity is created, stamp the lead with "SQL". When sales creates an opportunity, they see it as a sales-qualified lead.
   g. When the opportunity is won, change the stage to "Won".
   h. Is the opportunity lost? Is 'Lead Status' changed to "Disqualified"? Company type changed to "Competitor"? Then change the stage to "Disqualified".

"Companies that automate lead management see a 10% or more bump in revenue in six to nine months' time."

Strategic IC

This very simple setup will provide you with some of the essentials you need in marketing. It will allow you to know which leads to nurture and which not to nurture. It will also provide you with some direction on what to communicate in nurturing.

What I haven't covered yet is recycling leads that are lost or rejected from the queue. The ones that don't become SAL or Disqualified. In this simple model, you could simply turn them back to "Known", and reduce their scores.

What are the criteria for a marketing qualified lead (MQL)? Sales still wants to see every lead at Quintiq. So the criteria are very simple. We only keep absolute garbage or uncontactable leads out. This is the first small cut, which will allow me to make bigger cuts and roll out bigger improvements in the future.

Quintiq's first criteria for a Marketing Qualified Lead:
- A working email address and company name are available
- Or a phone number and company name are available

When a new email address is created in the automation platform, it's often due to a form fill. This means a confirmation email is sent. Thus we'll know if the email address bounces or not.

Automated Lead Assignment Process to Reduce Time to Contact

Quintiq now has a very elementary lead "management" process in place. One without service level agreements (SLA) or sophisticated logic on propensity to buy. But MQLs were still being pushed to a generic queue in the CRM. Inside sales around the world used a follow-the-sun principle to browse through the queue and manually assign leads to sales colleagues in any of the twelve business units around the world. On average, it took about forty-eight hours before someone followed up on a lead. Before the follow-the-sun principle, it took more than seventy-two hours. Leads that are assigned to the wrong individual have to be reassigned, which takes even longer. Time to automate things!

Of the twelve business units Quintiq has, six cover an industry vertical (e.g., rail or manufacturing). The other units have a regional orientation (e.g., China or Australia). Any lead from Australia goes to business units in Australia. Even rail companies. If a lead does not belong to a region, it is assigned to the appropriate industry-oriented business unit. Regional units often collaborate with industry-oriented units for their expertise.

> "There's a 400% difference following up with a lead within five minutes rather than ten. The success of follow-ups also depends on factors such as the time of day, the day of the week, response time, and how often you touch base. By no means should you harass leads, but you need to enroll them in lead nurturing campaigns that remind them of the value your company offers."

> *Hubspot*

The logic required for assigning should sound very straightforward for a marketing automation specialist. Quintiq already leverages a field to explicitly stamp the business unit based on who the lead is assigned to. Quintiq also uses this field in all their key reporting. A new field is created: "Inferred Business Unit". In the future, I would use interest scoring or other methods to distill the best-suited business unit, but right now I'm using the more simplistic setup below.

Is the country for the lead known? If not, use the inferred country. Does that country match a regional business unit? If so, change the value for "Inferred Business Unit" to that business unit. If not, go to the next workflow. The next workflow looks at the last download. Since Quintiq's whitepapers live in virtual folders that match an industry, it's pretty simple. Otherwise, you could do partial matches on filenames. Is there no download? Then use the next workflow. That next workflow looks at which part of the site was browsed.

If the lead visited at least three pages within a certain virtual directory, then assign it to the business unit associated with that industry. But it can well be that this results in multiple matches. So I order by business unit priority, which can be a bit arbitrary.

Every business unit now has its own queue in CRM. I update the process that syncs leads to the generic queue when MQL is stamped. It now syncs to any of the twelve queues based on the value in the field "Inferred Business Unit".

> *"Over 99% of leads are now assigned to the correct business unit with more than 99% accuracy."*

Within every business unit, all sales representatives monitor their queue and assign leads to themselves. Queues should be empty as soon as possible. Rob even implements and reports on an age field for "Days in Queue". Over 99% of leads are now assigned to the correct business unit with more than 99% accuracy. And as a result, some leads are now being followed up on within moments after they became MQL. This drives much higher conversion rates.

Basic Nurturing and Scoring to Distinguish Hot from Cold Leads

There's an introduction session for new employees with each of the five founders every month. Quintiq has an inspiring chief operations officer, who I first met during such an introduction session. He presented some interesting marketing and sales tactics. There was only one thing I did not agree on. He said that they got roughly one deal for every one hundred new names generated by marketing. So he initiated a project for the marketing team in Kuala Lumpur to double new name generation from 5,000 to 10,000 per year, as those efforts would result in roughly doubling sales.

> "Businesses who nurture leads make 50% more sales at a cost 33% less than nonnurtured prospects."
>
> *Strategic IC*

You're now thinking, "That makes sense. Why would you not agree with that?" Well, he has a point, but in real life, doubling your top of funnel (TOFU) doesn't necessarily double your won deals at the bottom of your funnel. Those of you with digital advertising experience know that the average price per lead increases when you need more leads. You need to go to ever more lengths to find those last gems in the vastness of the internet. And the more you broaden the net, the lower the quality of your leads. So maintaining the 1-to-100 ratio will be difficult in real life.

"The use of lead nurturing through marketing automation saw 15%–20% of potential buyers that were not ready to purchase converted to sales."

Protocol80

Let's provide you with some more context before describing my solution. A typical buyer of Quintiq is a real business-to-business (B2B) buyer. It takes a decision-making unit (DMU) at a company at least several months to complete its buying journey. In sales jargon, you can consider a Quintiq software license a "Big Ticket Deal."

That's why I set up Quintiq's first nurture campaigns—not to convert inquiries to MQLs but to support the entire buyer journey. This is to maintain or improve the end-to-end conversion of one in one hundred. Nurturing is *not* reserved for only getting MQLs. There's a 50% chance you're currently only leveraging nurturing for only this. A very big missed opportunity!

"Nurturing is not reserved for only turning your inquiries into marketing qualified leads. You're likely missing out!"

Quintiq does not have any active nurture programs. And I want to facilitate the entire buyer journey and sales process. Simplifying the journey to just three main phases is the first step. I call the phases early, middle, and late. They roughly resemble SiriusDecisions' buying phases: Awareness, Consideration, and Decision.

Awareness is for someone who still needs to become aware that they might have a problem. For Quintiq, that could be like, "Is your logistics process leaving money on the table?" During the awareness phase, the DMU is searching for possible solutions. Build more distribution points? Purchase more trucks? Optimize logistics planning with smarter software? At the end of the awareness phase, a DMU concludes they should probably need to optimize their supply chain with smart software.

It's during the consideration phase that they want to learn more about this solution, how others implemented it, and which vendors should make the shortlist. They also investigate budgets and planning. At the end of the consideration phase, the DMU concludes they should go ahead. In Quintiq's case, they are committed to purchasing and implementing a supply chain planning and optimization platform.

In the decision phase, the DMU selects the vendor from a shortlist. Who's going to provide us with the optimization platform? I often hear that content creation is seen as the biggest hurdle for lead nurturing. Creating a whitepaper can be very costly, either in internal hours or external costs. Imagine what a full-blown nurture program would cost you? I need a scalable way to proof and fund nurture programs.

A colleague of mine, the content marketing manager, once came up with an idea for content creation based on something she picked up at a conference (The Content Marketing Pyramid™). She adapted it to a content pyramid for Quintiq. After some iterations, I came up with what I now call the nurture content pyramid.

NURTURE CONTENT PYRAMID

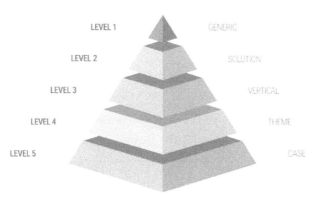

LEVEL 1	GENERIC
LEVEL 2	SOLUTION
LEVEL 3	VERTICAL
LEVEL 4	THEME
LEVEL 5	CASE

The top of the pyramid has generic nurture programs. The bottom has very specific niche-related nurture programs, which are the most relevant to the recipients and thus have higher conversion rates.

The top of the pyramid is for your company's core. Everybody has a planning puzzle to solve. Creating and leveraging content around that main theme ensures that every lead has some content to consume.

But solving a production planning puzzle is very different than a logistics puzzle. Engaging with content on logistics problems will resonate much better with prospects that have a logistics challenge. That will result in higher conversion rates. But that means we must also have a separate logistics, workforce, and production nurture program.

As soon as we know enough about a lead, we can automatically send them to the nurture program that best fits the lead. You can imagine that producing metals is very different from assembling cars. And producing aluminum is very different from producing copper. So at the bottom of the pyramid, there should be copper-specific pieces of content (e.g., whitepapers). A fifth level could be case specific. Basically, a case study!

I decide to create the main overarching nurture program. That way, every lead can be nurtured. And I decide to create a production program, a metals program, and a copper program. Together with Daniella, a marketer at the metals business unit, we gather all available content. And we decide what a logical order for the content would be. We don't have enough content on copper to create a nurture program for copper. But by combining copper content with content from the levels above (e.g., metals and production), we'll have a copper nurture program in no time! The team in Kuala Lumpur now starts to create the required texts and images for the nurture emails.

"When innovating, use the scalable mindset!"

Meanwhile, I'll let you in on a secret. I chose to create one program for each level of the pyramid, as I anticipated that conversion rates would improve within every lower level of the pyramid. I'm already preparing the business case for a massive endeavor—the creation of all the missing content and nurture programs! This also meets my criteria for scalability. Every time I innovate, it should work not only today but also in the future. I call it "the scalable mindset." You might spend a bit more effort right now, but it will save you from a lot of redesigning in the future.

With nurture programs in place to engage with leads, it's time to measure that engagement and determine which leads are hot and which leads are not. This is where lead scoring comes in. I've seen so many poor lead-scoring attempts. Let's do Quintiq justice and come up with something proper, considering it's 2013. Most people decide to focus scoring on behavior. But that results in a higher score for more active leads. This assumes that more active people have a higher propensity to buy. To be brutally honest, that's a bit shortsighted, right?

Lead Scoring Dimensions

Without any research or data to back up my assumptions, I'm thinking about four scoring dimensions to at least come to a better way of predicting propensity to buy at this point:

- Demographics/firmographics versus behavior
- Implicit versus explicit data
- Active versus latent (= proactive versus reactive)
- Special

Typically, the top 1% of scores in the system receive three stars. The next tier of 2%–5% receives two stars. The next 15% receive one star. The rest of the database has no stars.

How would I prioritize two leads with the same score? One might have a recent score buildup, while the other lead may be several months old and already decaying in score. The answer lies within relative urgency. The score build-up in the recent past. The top 1% most urgent receive three flames. And so on.

Marketo Engage uses this system of stars and flames. Same with their Salesforce integration. Within Marketo Engage, I was able to define the exact thresholds for stars and flames to fit Quintiq's needs.

	Implicit		Explicit	
	Latent	Active	Latent	Active
Behavior	Opens an email that was sent to him or her.	Attends a webinar or downloads an ungated document.	Answers a direct question in a sent survey.	Submits a request for a proposal form.
Demo-graphics	A web page visit results in an inferred company name through reversed IP look-up.	Clicking one of three industry-related links in an email suggests the company is active in that industry.	The lead's data is appended through third-party integration.	The company name is provided through a form fill.
Special	One month of total inactivity.		Third-party intent data is used to enrich the lead's profile.	

This Chapter's Challenges	This Chapter's Solutions
Leads are manually assigned to sales, which takes several days, which results in cold leads.	Over 99% of leads are now assigned to the correct business unit with more than 99% accuracy through simple workflows in the marketing automation platform.
Marketing's efforts cannot be attributed to sales successes.	A new but simplistic lead management process keeps track of where leads are in the sales process.
There is no way to distinguish hot from cold leads. Traditionally, sales doesn't fully trust marketing yet and wants to make sure every lead is handed over (hot and cold).	The new lead management process allows for an unnoticeable cut, where the marketing automation platform decides when to send to sales. Basic scoring provides a temperature of leads sent.
A product or solution could solve any puzzle, but prospects want to hear it can solve their unique challenge.	The nurture content pyramid allows for easy assembling of nurture programs to be as relevant as possible in a scalable and affordable way.
How to source enough budget for nurture programs?	

FULL SERVICE OR FULL OF CRAP?

My journey in marketing automation didn't start at Quintiq in late 2012. Together with my best friend and fellow student, I started EventTrips back in 2002. It was a website with packaged trips to festivities like La Tomatina in Bunol or Carnival in Venice. Edwin and I learned to program in PHP and to use MySQL queries to build the EventTrips website. And of course, the website needed to pop up on Google, which led us to search engine marketing, something I also helped other companies with during my Bachelor's in Business.

It wasn't a big surprise that I got my first job after graduating at a full-service internet agency instead of pursuing a career in finance. At Prezent Internet, I was selling and consulting on custom-built websites, e-commerce, and search engine marketing between 2007 and 2009.

I kept learning more about online marketing and started working at TiasNimbas Business School in 2009. TiasNimbas is one of the Financial Times' best MBA business schools in the world. This is when I really started my career in marketing automation.

Selecting a €40,000 master of business administration (MBA) just isn't the same as putting a pair of Nikes in a webshop's shopping basket. I started searching the internet for examples of more complex purchases. I stumbled on concepts like buying journeys, buyer personas, and event-driven marketing.

> *"Selecting a €40,000 MBA just isn't the same as putting a pair of Nikes in your online shopping basket!"*

Together with the web content manager at TiasNimbas, we were the only online marketers in a group of eight offline marketers. The web content manager came over from the United States. We shared an office, which allowed me to practice my English daily for more than two years.

For some courses, I was buying leads from a Dutch online agency, but for most courses, I used the website to generate leads through course brochure downloads. I came up with the first nurture program, though without any technology yet.

Through ads on Google Adwords, I generated course brochure downloads, which we then invited for an example class. All the people who applied for the example class were then handed over to 'study advisors,' a fancier name than sales. I quickly realized different types and/or formats of content would fit different buying stages. Luckily, I stumbled on a model for this.

The Content Marketing Matrix
By

The web content manager and I explored new technology for the new website. That was the first time I learned more about relevant technology, such as Marketo Engage and Sitecore OMS. Unfortunately, I couldn't stay for the implementation because I was scouted by a B2B Marketing Agency.

Milestone Marketing was a small agency with about fifteen to twenty people split into two groups. There were seven consultants for digital marketing, including myself, my manager, and the owner. And there were about ten people in execution (e.g., social media, email marketing, web development, etc.).

On my second day, I joined the owner to prepare and host a workshop about elevator pitches. We sold the workshop, but had to come up with the content on the spot. Not too long after, he and I flew to the United Kingdom for an event. The event was hosted by someone who made marketing profitable. And he was teaching others how to do that too. He spoke at events and pitched attendees to sign up for a members-only website, where he shared content. He then hosted paid events like the one we attended. And we learned quite a few things there. I was most impressed by how he managed to sell ten website optimization packages, each for $5,000, in just one minute by creating scarcity. At the end of the event, he also sold five VIP trips to his mansion for a three-day private course, each for $50,000. Every step in his marketing funnel made a profit instead of costing money.

My regular work at Milestone was mostly project based and focused on buyer personas, buyer journeys, digital marketing transformation, marketing automation, and social media.

Back in 2010, companies were still struggling with how to leverage social media in B2B. I was wondering why certain content went viral and why other content didn't. I started researching viral content. And I kept blogging about social media posts that went viral, especially the funny ones. Who can't remember the Tipp-Ex videos with a bear? After a while, I started noticing similarities and patterns, and I created a model for increasing your chances of creating a viral post. It was the first marketing-related model I ever put on paper. So don't expect too much from it. And it's not even about marketing automation, but I thought it would be interesting to include in this story.

The Social Media Sharing Model, Diederik Martens - 2010

Which bottlenecks need to be addressed when using social media in marketing campaigns? Please note the illustration below is the original and authentic, and thus low-res, illustration from 2010.

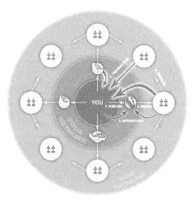

1. Publish

One could decide to use social media for a campaign (e.g., an open house for a university). One of the reasons could be to save on media spending. First, make sure that the company's social media presence is already established and there's frequent interaction with the network. The open house could be mentioned on Twitter, Facebook, and/or LinkedIn. A clear call to action should be communicated (e.g., a hyperlink to a registration form). It's important to publish outside your profile as well. Try to find other locations to publish too. But watch out! Don't try to sell too much.

2. Share

The idea of the model is that your network will share your message with their network. This enables you to reach people outside your direct network without enormous paid ads. People in your network also act as ambassadors. **Bottleneck:** Why would anyone take the trouble to share your message?

3. Reshare

Real success is only achieved when a campaign goes far beyond your connections. This is when your message gets reshared to your network's networks. This creates large exposure with minimal media costs. But an investment will most likely be necessary to address the following bottleneck. **Bottleneck:** Why would someone outside your network (who doesn't know you) take the trouble to reshare your message?

4. Transaction

I assume your goals go beyond pure branding. Exposure alone doesn't help you sell products or services. There needs to be a transaction (e.g., downloading of a brochure, purchase, or registration). But when a message gets reshared frequently, it could become difficult for someone who doesn't know you to find you. So make sure people can still find you even when your message gets reshared (e.g., through a hyperlink).

Bottleneck: How would you direct someone to a transaction (without pushing too much)?

Bottleneck: Why would someone who doesn't know you be willing to start a transaction with you?

5. Interaction

Back to social media basics: It's about maintaining real relationships, based on bidirectional communication. So be sure to interact with the newly acquired network contacts.

Bottleneck: Where will you interact with them (which platform)?

Bottlenecks

There are many more bottlenecks to address in many of the subprocesses at each stage. But the main idea is to understand the potential bottlenecks at each stage of the resharing process. A funny video, something competitive, or a reward could be all that's needed for someone to share your message.

After using the social media sharing model with a customer of Milestone, I was asked by Milestone to run a project for a company, called Woonzorg. A company that focused on housing for seniors. They previously identified five different personas. One of the personas was "the prepper." He or she is about fifty-five years old and is already thinking about moving to a new home that is better suited for older people. Other personas included nature enthusiasts, city center enthusiasts, or personas looking for a place to rest and relax. Woonzorg typically levered old media to promote the opening of new locations. They wanted to go more digital, but they had no idea where to communicate which message. Together with the customer's team, I prepared interviews for the "a place to rest and relax" persona. We wanted to validate three things:

- Does the buyer journey indeed look like we internally imagined it?
- Which questions does the persona have at each stage of the journey?
- Which channels does the persona use to get questions answered?

"One of the strongest areas in which marketing automation can make a difference, according to survey results, is during the onboarding of new accounts."

SiriusDecisions

We split up the interviews for customers and potential customers in different regions. I jumped in the car and booked a hotel in Friesland, the North of the Netherlands. I interviewed several people and validated their buyer journey. We mostly focus on the left part of the journey, targeting prospects. Though it is equally important to do the same exercise for the right part, the customer lifecycle.

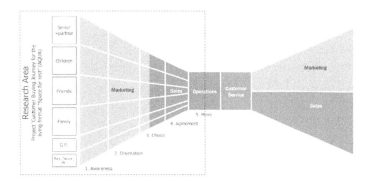

We also looked at the different influencers. And we looked at how much of an influence they were at each stage. And finally, we looked at the keyword/question for each persona at each stage. This resulted in the following visual I had to come up with.

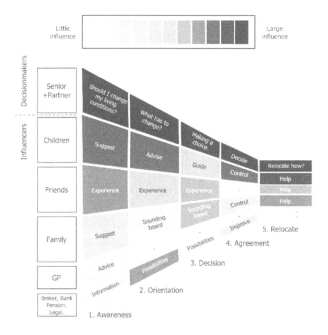

But how did I come up with the key question and theme for each persona stage? I came up with the idea to use mind maps.

Below is an example of a mind map for the second stage, "Orientation".

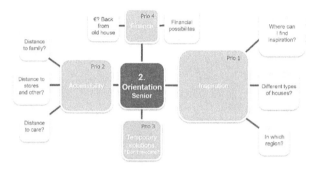

After validating the key questions for each persona at each buyer stage, we asked which channels they used to find answers to their questions. We then looked at what content the customer already had available. We then determined the content gap. We discovered they still had quite some content to create. We prioritized the new content based on the level of importance of each key question at each stage. That way, we insured that they first created the content that has the highest impact on the buyer journey (compared to the effort involved in creating it). We used a simple matrix for this.

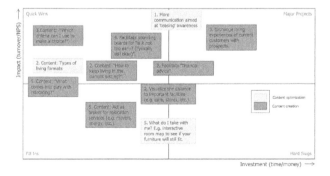

Another interesting project at Milestone in 2011 was a daughter of Danone. I helped them with several topics, including the selection of a marketing automation platform for the Dutch branch of the group. Where the United Kingdom was leveraging Oracle Eloqua, we were evaluating Marketo Engage or Sitecore DMS. I talked to many stakeholders about how we would enable sales, which visited general practitioners and doctors, with marketing automation. Back then, the focus was more on customer profiling than on engaging with those profiles. For that reason, and because they also already had Oracle Eloqua in-house, I advised them to choose Sitecore DMS, a platform that was also used by another daughter of Danone.

Looking back, the most-fun projects were at Q-Park, a company with almost six thousand parking facilities throughout Europe. Together with my main stakeholder, who was responsible for digital transformation at Q-park, we worked on a variety of projects, some of them with the HR department. I helped them set up social media guidelines for employees (that was a thing back then). We even had a video created for employees. And we created a social media escalation model. That way, the customer care team had a decision tree for when to respond or not respond to social mentions. I also organized a LinkedIntakeLunch for Q-Park staff to get their professional picture taken. Together with experts and tips, people updated their profiles over lunch.

One of my last projects at Milestone was at KPN, one of the biggest and oldest Dutch telecom providers. I mostly did back-office work for a Milestone colleague who was in the lead, but I enjoyed a small project where I was asked to shape the future for digital campaigning. KPN also taught me that larger companies with long histories and prior acquisitions are slow, inefficient, and ineffective in digital transformation. That's not to say that KPN was doing a bad job. But compared to smaller companies or even start-ups, things were going painfully slow. I learned to create and pitch mini business cases, pitch pilots, and scale up successes—something that would become a vital element in the Chaploop™ I designed many years later.

Something else that caught my attention at Milestone was that marketing leaders kept asking me what the next big innovation would be for them and how they could grow their (digital) marketing maturity. I thought that with over fifty years of marketing education and with almost ten years of online marketing, someone should have already created something for this. But I was unable to find anything. So I started puzzling over it in my personal time.

I came up with a model. Little did I know that quite a few elements would make it into the Chaploop™, my MarTech innovation business growth model, many years later.

The Digital Marketing Maturity Growth Model, Diederik Martens - 2011

Axis
The horizontal axis indicates a company's maturity. The maturity is divided into five levels: ad hoc, repeatable, defined, managed, and optimizing. The vertical axis represents the (financial) value for the business.

Growth
The growth lies in the combination of the two axes. The growth curve can be recognized as a common S-curve from the "old" marketing literature. In the beginning, growth is slow and the effort is high. After this, everything accelerates (little effort and big impact). In the end, it becomes increasingly difficult to achieve additional business value.

Circles of Focus Areas
The circles are the focus areas of the model. The size of the filled circles represents the internal focus and attention that the company has on the focus areas. The size of the empty circles represents the attention and focus necessary for the next period in the growth plan of the company. The five focus areas are communication, omnichannel, sales enablement, customer insight, and marketing intelligence.

Company Profile
The filled area between all five focus areas is the "position" that the company holds. The model can be used as a quick scan. And it can be used to benchmark different companies.

Other
The growth directions always focus on the growth curve (S-curve). This balances business value, effort, and focus reasonably. All values are obtained by a questionnaire (answers in scores).

The figure on the next page shows a screenshot from a company that I assessed. You'll notice some slight differences in naming.

Maturity	Focus Areas
Ad Hoc	**Communications**
Marketing is carried out chaotically. This often means that there's no marketing department. Often agencies are used for incidental work. Marketing is more luck than skill.	The way of communicating (e.g., thought leadership, outside-in, content, structure, timing, and relevance).
Repeatable	**Omnichannel**
Processes are repeatable. Often there are only a few people involved with marketing and some methods are documented. One can reasonably make decisions for future action based on past results.	Use, selection, and (seamless) integration of channels, target audience relative to channel, and interaction.
Defined	**Sales Enablement**
Marketing processes are well established within the organization. A marketing department has several areas of expertise.	The way marketing "blends" with sales. Are bidirectional service-level agreements (SLA) established with sales (marketing automation, lead nurturing, etc.)?
Managed	**Customer Insights**
Marketing has a prominent role in the organization. Results are monitored and adjusted when necessary. Marketing works with dashboards and key performance indicators.	Customer-360, social CRM, customer obsession, and knowing what moves and engages the customer.
Optimized	**Marketing Intelligence**
This is the fine-tuning. One can improve detailed processes in a specialized way. Management can make data-driven decisions.	What is the competition doing? How is the market organized? Understanding opportunities and threats.

Marketing Maturity Growth Model

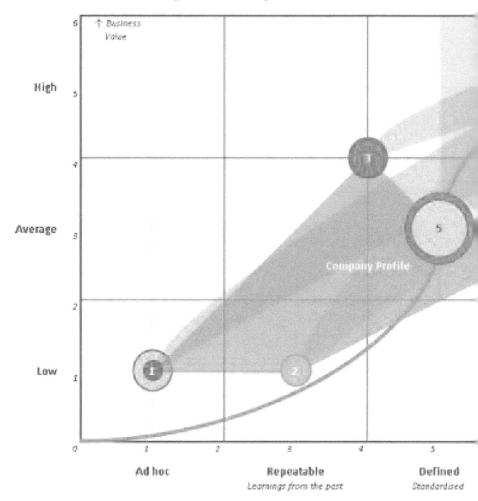

Growth

© Diederik Martens 2011

Legenda
Communications
Channels
Salesenablement
Customer insights
Marketing intelligence

*Company focal areas(es)
with circle sizes (1-5)*

Left of the line?
Grow by maturing

Right of the line?
Grow by adding more
businessvalue

Marketing
Maturity →

7   8   9   10

Managed   **Optimizing**
Measuring quality and improving   *Finetuning*

Milestone was also on a very ambitious growth path. Maybe too ambitious. We were doing great in consulting back then. But all the execution staff were working for a single client. And that client left. That resulted in 60% of the staff not having any paid work. My fellow consultants and I were consulting on different topics than the expertise of the execution staff. That's when the ship sank. I remember this time as very stressful.

Luckily for me, Milestone restarted but only with the consulting business. After a while, it just didn't feel the same anymore. A lot of great colleagues left. And I was still feeling insecure about the company's future.

And, as you've probably noticed in this chapter, I constantly had to quickly come up with or invent things for customers because we didn't have any experience with what we sold yet. Back then, I thought this was business as usual for consultants. Friends at other big, well-known consulting firms confirmed this. But I didn't feel comfortable with this. I didn't want my customers to be my guinea pigs. I wanted to help customers become successful through leveraging proven best practices instead. This belief became the anchor for the core values of the agency I founded many years later.

> *"I really wanted to help customers become successful through leveraging proven best-practices instead."*

I sat down with my wife in the summer of 2012, right after our second daughter was born and right before we got the key to our newly built house. I was unable to combine the busy family life and the long hours and travel for Milestone. Combined with my doubts about Milestone, we decided it would be best to start looking for that new job. It turned out to be one of the best career choices I made, and I ended up at Quintiq just a few months later.

This Chapter's Challenges	This Chapter's Solutions
Choosing a Master of Business Administration comes with a longer and more complex buyer journey than purchasing a pair of Nikes. How can I align with the buyer's journey?	The Content Marketing Matrix from Smart Insights helped us decide which type of content would work well in which buyer stage.
Why would people share your content? And how would we be able to generate more new names as a result?	I created a social media sharing model after a long stretch of blogging about viral campaigns.
Marketing leaders kept asking me about what their next step in marketing maturity would be.	I came up with a Digital Marketing Maturity Growth Model, which can also be used as an assessment and to benchmark companies.
How would I be able to verify buyer journey stages?	I used interviews and color gradings to visualize the level of importance of stages, personas, and questions.
How can I define the key theme for each persona stage?	For each intersection of persona and stage, I summarized the interviews in mind maps.
How should I prioritize the creation of missing content?	I used a priority matrix to balance impact versus effort to prioritize the creation of missing content.
How should I deal with learning on the job versus bluffing on the job?	Core values and integrity became a big part of my new work ethic.

MARTECH INNOVATION WITHOUT A BUDGET

Back to Quintiq. It's the start of 2014 and the second of my three years at Quintiq. It's 2:00 p.m. in the Netherlands, and Jeff, our CMO, calls me from the Philadelphia office. A sales representative is trying to close a multimillion-dollar deal—one of the biggest deals for that business unit. The deal is almost in the pocket, but there's a catch. The prospect needs their CEO to sign the papers, but their CEO unexpectedly asked for a reference visit. The food market is new to Quintiq, so we don't have any relevant references. It can easily take a few weeks to set up a C-Level meeting. And competitors can come back with more aggressive pricing while we are waiting for the reference visit. Jeff was thinking about a small project that I pitched a few weeks earlier, something I called "prospect portals."

Prospect Portals

I spent eight hours turning my draft concept portal into a live prospect portal. I add the prospect's logo and an introduction text from the sales representative. I also add his picture. And I add shortcuts to relevant content. This includes a reference video from a steel manufacturer. I make the Marketo Engage landing page touch responsive on tablets with a carousel script. It allows the viewer to easily swipe through the content. Later that evening, I send the link to the prospect portal to Jeff and go to bed.

The next afternoon, I receive a call from Jeff. He sounds excited. "We won the deal! Everybody is talking about your prospect portals." I cannot yet imagine that this small technical innovation is the start of a better alignment with sales at Quintiq.

The sales representative calls me the next day. He tells me he has several more late-stage opportunities. So I sit down with my team to see how we can optimize the process of prospect portal generation. We build five more portals. It takes us about four hours to build each portal. But we're not satisfied because the current process is not scalable. It doesn't fit my Scalable Mindset philosophy, and we are expecting more requests soon, especially from the Northern American business unit.

We decide to build a master prospect portal, a portal with a dummy logo that contains all the content we have available. We use variables for the logo so we can easily update it. And we can simply remove the content we don't need. That will be much quicker than adding content from scratch. We also create a page that displays all the available content, an explanation of prospect portals, and a request form. Through this page, any sales representative can easily request a portal. The team, which now also includes my brother-in-law Maarten, is now able to deliver a new prospect portal in about one hour. Just in time, as news travels fast and we're getting more requests.

The team and I are at Quintiq's quarterly company business update when we're confronted with a slide full of logos. These logos represent the customers we signed this quarter. The logos are very familiar to us. We open our notebooks and start digging into the data. We built about forty portals, of which twenty-four received traffic from the prospects—the same twenty-four logos on the slide! A 100% match! That value is far from significant, but it makes for great spaghetti statistics.

"All the prospect portals that were visited turned into deals. That makes for some great spaghetti statistics!"

News of the successes travels faster and also reaches our Australian business unit. They even receive calls from prospects to mention that they appreciate the effort Quintiq takes to build these portals and that is one of the reasons they chose Quintiq. The team and I sit down and think about further improvements.

Marketo Engage automatically recognizes leads and allows us to conditionally show a form or not. We leverage this functionality to only show a form to leads we do not yet recognize. This allows us to identify new people within the decision-making unit of the prospect. Why would somebody at a prospect visit the prospect portal if they didn't have any role in the opportunity? If they are not a decision maker, they are at least influencers. Some deals are more sensitive than others. We improve security and add passwords to some prospect portals for enhanced security.

We are also thinking about making the portals even more personal. We record a simple introduction video with a local sales representative. In the video, he explains why Quintiq built a customized page for the visitor. The video appears as if it was recorded for that specific prospect, but in fact, it can be used for different prospects. When we analyze the data, we see that portals with videos outperform portals with only a photo.

Quintiq also participates in public requests for proposals (RFPs). Quintiq and different competitors each send their best proposal after a briefing.

UNITED STATES POSTAL SERVICE

ough this page you can access a variety of selected materials,
:: Case Studies, Testimonials, Management Briefings, Videos,
3 Demo Screenshots.

u can also check:

Quintiq
Quintiq - Logistics
Quintiq - Postal & Express

se feel free to contact me if you have any further questions.

 Tim Kehrer
Sr. Account Executive

 Steve Wallace
Inside Sales Specialist

RFPs often come with a silence period after submitting. RFPs follow strict processes. This means sales is limited to no engagement with the prospect. There is no way to provide additional context or influence the process. Welcome prospect portals! During the silence period, we are still able to monitor if the prospect portals are visited and who visits. We can even publish additional content on the portals. We can't notify the prospect about the new content, but if they take the initiative to visit the portal, they would be able to see the new content. All within the strict RFP rules of engagement.

In the end, prospect portals become mandatory at Quintiq when an opportunity reaches the 30% stage. And every sales representative records his or her own prospect portal video introduction.

Don't Simply Execute a Suggested Solution—Ask Why First

Another day, another request to the marketing operations team at Quintiq. If you are a marketing automation specialist or working in marketing operations like me, you'll probably recognize requests like: "Can you create a new field for me?" Instead of describing their problem, many people tend to prescribe a solution to their problem.

> *"If you're in operations, you'll recognize that many people tend to prescribe a solution rather than describe their problem."*

Imagine your colleague went to the facility manager to ask them to crank up the air-conditioning because he or she is sweating. In this scenario, your colleague is proposing a solution. But your colleague is not an office climate expert. Will lowering the air-conditioning temperature reduce sweat? And maybe there are more people in the building than just your colleague. How will the proposed solution scale and impact others? A better way would be for your colleague to describe the problem faced. "I'm sweating." The office manager would align with an expert, who might conclude they are getting too much direct sunlight through the window. The solution might be to close the shutters, something completely different than cranking up the air-conditioning, which could result in many colleagues needing to wear jackets to stay warm.

The solution someone once shared with me is to ask, "Why?" five times. "Why do you want this new field?" The goal is not to come across as being difficult but to ensure the solution you design solves the underlying problem. Asking why also enables you to make sure the solution helps others and scales into the future. If you don't, you'll likely be applying short-term fix upon short-term fix instead of addressing the real challenges. You won't be able to quickly innovate and grow.

"**Five whys** (or 5 whys) is an iterative interrogative technique used to explore the cause-and-effect relationships underlying a particular problem.

The primary goal of the technique is to determine the root cause of a defect or problem by repeating the question, "Why?" Each answer forms the basis of the next question. The "five" in the name derives from an anecdotal observation on the number of iterations needed to resolve the problem.

Not all problems have a single root cause. If one wishes to uncover multiple root causes, the method must be repeated, asking a different sequence of questions each time.

The method provides no hard and fast rules about what lines of questions to explore or how long to continue the search for additional root causes. Thus, even when the method is closely followed, the outcome still depends on the knowledge and persistence of the people involved.

The technique was originally developed by Sakichi Toyoda and was used within the Toyota Motor Corporation during the evolution of its manufacturing methodologies."

Wikipedia.org

Multilingual Nurture Campaigns

My team now supports all the Quintiq business units across the globe. We have 6:00 a.m. calls with Australia and 8:00 p.m. calls with the United States. We now have over 250 different pieces of content created by the online marketing team in Kuala Lumpur. Some are available in up to eight different languages. But up till now, all our nurture programs are in English only.

We take inventory of which content is being used in nurture programs. We check which content is available in other languages. We then check whether we have enough coverage in a certain language to justify a nurture program.

We select all languages for the nurture program with at least 85% coverage. And we put anything with 65% coverage on a backlog. We then check with the different business units to see whether the main topic is interesting enough for that language. One might assume there's interest based on the fact the translation is available, but we could be wrong. A few missing translations are selected to be translated. For these pieces of content and the other selected content, we ask for the promotional texts (e.g., email texts) to be translated too. Within just a few weeks, we have our fifteen nurture programs live in multiple languages. Most of the programs at the top of the Nurture Content Pyramid are available in all eight languages.

In the past weeks, we were already running some tests that showed much higher conversation rates for translated content. We noticed that engaging audiences in both their native language and English doesn't result in higher conversions. We see higher conversion rates when addressing a lead in a single language, preferably their own language. Together with Lorenzo Corea, a regional marketeer in Italy, we test solely engaging in Italian in combination with one of the new translated nurture programs. This resulted in higher conversion rates and a significant increase in revenue attribution.

We then create this Marketo Engage page for the rest of the organization to show and promote which nurture programs are available.

There are so many ways to technically address multiple languages in marketing automation. One way is to set up a separate program for each language. Some platforms, which integrate with the most common marketing automation platforms, can ingest full campaign texts and connect them to translators. When you approve the translations, the platform automatically creates a new cloned campaign with the translated texts.

We already have our translation processes, so we can set up any process we like. We choose to have our content campaigns be multilingual and automatically select the right language. This also means we do not need extra nurture programs. Our Marketo Engage nurture programs do not use emails directly but refer to other programs, which we call content programs. These programs contain the logic for each piece of content.

Centralizing Your Content in Content Programs

A content program is a container for anything related to a piece of content (e.g., a whitepaper). When someone downloads the whitepaper on your corporate website, they become a member of that content program. And the marketing automation platform sends the delivery email with the download. When sales sends a marketing email with that same whitepaper through CRM, the recipient also becomes a member. And if someone engages with that content through nurturing, they also become a member. That way, we can manage, monitor, and measure anything that happens with a specific piece of content. And we can also prevent pitching the same content twice.

> *"A content program is a container for a specific piece of content (e.g., a whitepaper) designed to manage, monitor, and measure any engagement, and it prevents pitching content that was already consumed."*

We have a field for "Preferred Language". When empty, it is stamped with the inferred language. This is based on the website domain a lead visits. But if a lead downloads a whitepaper in a specific language (not English), then it is overwritten. Further overwrites are protected, except for updates sales makes in CRM or if the lead fills out the field in a form. That way, we ensure the best possible preferred language for a lead.

The content program has an if/else statement for every language available for that content so that the preferred language is used. If the preferred language is not available, it will either not be sent or the English version will be sent. This depends on the content and the region of the lead. This is to ensure single-language engagement for regions that apply that approach.

Agile Marketing

Later that year, Rob introduces biweekly "sprints." The sales operations team and the marketing operations team both plan what miniprojects and tasks they want to complete for each of the next two weeks. This allows us to show what we both deliver every two weeks. The idea is borrowed from agile software development but without a backlog. It's a helpful method as both our operations teams are in between business and technology. Agile SCRUM is a methodology widely used in software development today. All of these are ideas that could provide (user) value or be put on a big to-do list, which is called the backlog. Every cycle takes about two to three weeks. These are called sprints. Each sprint starts with sprint planning. The team selects items from the backlog to deliver in the upcoming sprint. Each item is something that provides independent value to the business. So if one stopped developing, there is still a working product at the end of each sprint.

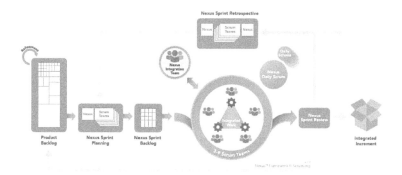

The team "pokers" for every sprint item to estimate how much effort the item would take. The effort is expressed in story points. These refer to comparable items (from the past). Typically, one story point equals four hours of work. Each sprint ends with a sprint demo to showcase what was delivered for the business. And during a sprint review, the team reflects on the completed sprint and discusses what they can learn and take into the next sprint.

This Chapter's Challenges	This Chapter's Solutions
How can marketing support sales at the end of the buyer's journey?	Prospect portals allow for discovering more people in the decision-making unit. They provide extra content during RFPs. They provide a personalized experience.
How to ensure that solutions truly solve the real problem in a scalable way?	Ask "Why?" at least five times to unravel the underlying cause and effect.
How to further increase nurture conversion rates?	Multilingual nurture programs allow for single language engagement, which drives higher conversion rates.
How to manage, monitor, and measure any engagement with a specific piece of content, regardless of channel? How to prevent pitching content that was already consumed?	Content programs in MAP will track members in a centralized fashion. They contain teaser emails (gated and ungated), delivery emails, logic, etc.
How to bridge business and technology? How to show(case) progress of the operations team and its value to the business?	Implement something similar to Agile SCRUM and start to work in sprints.

A SHORT LESSON IN MARKETING AUTOMATION HISTORY

Thus far, marketing automation has been the source of many of my team's successes at Quintiq and my personal successes as well. But what makes marketing automation so powerful? I will have to take you through how marketing automation evolved.

Companies have been trying to sell their services and products for a very long time. There are usually a lot of other companies to compete with. Every company wants to outsmart the others. It made a lot of sense to bring technology into marketing.

When radio and television found their way to the masses, companies finally found a "cheap" way to reach bigger audiences. And they found a way to target audiences based on segments (e.g., commercials during specific television shows). The rise of personal computers and the internet provided companies with a way to target individuals in large quantities. One-to-one marketing at scale was born. That's when we started to think about automating some of the processes.

After the new millennium, there was an uprise in new cloud technologies. Though they were still expensive and didn't have many endorsements at the time. Eloqua, currently owned by Oracle, is one of the first successful platforms. But it still required heavy IT investment to operate. Challengers like Marketo Engage, currently owned by Adobe, turned things around. Instead of being designed by IT, the new platforms were designed by marketers.

The software industry (B2B) was one of the first industries to adopt marketing automation while consumer brands stayed focused on online advertising and optimizing ad-bidding. Silicon Valley, the Bay Area, San Francisco—that's where a lot was happening. Somehow, start-ups found it easy to incorporate marketing automation from the start, while established companies were still struggling to implement automation in their ancient company processes. It didn't take too long before marketing automation spread from the west coast of the United States and reached the east coast. And then it found its way to Canada. It did take at least another one or two years to find its way into Europe, starting in the United Kingdom and the Netherlands. Companies like Planon Software and Quintiq were among the early adopters in the Netherlands.

The number of emails, ads, and posts was exploding. Potential customers became overwhelmed with impressions. They start to think about closing their inboxes. We've realized that we've entered an era of customer centricity. Especially after the recession of 2008.

We must be relevant to our audiences. They even started to expect that from us. This feeling strengthens in the ten years following the recession as the masses get accustomed to instant drone delivery from Amazon and Netflix TV suggestions.

"In order to be relevant, one must first understand."

You can only be relevant to somebody if you also understand them. This, in my opinion, turned out to be one of the biggest game changers for the adoption of marketing automation. Companies that successfully leveraged marketing automation beat their competitors that didn't.

Other industries soon followed. After the software industry, we saw high-tech and manufacturing adopting marketing automation. Then we saw business services, education, and healthcare follow. And later we saw logistics and finance. And not only in B2B. Marketing automation also found its way to B2C.

For many industries, marketing automation has become as vital for marketing as CRM is for sales. Without it, you simply wouldn't be able to win against the competition. But there are still many industries where marketing automation can provide early adopters the competitive edge necessary to become the winners of tomorrow.

Marketing technology is becoming cheaper to purchase and implement. Why? The supply is growing. Scott Brinker publishes a MarTech landscape every year. It has grown from a few dozen to over seven thousand platforms in the past ten years. Competition is fierce, and lower price points allow more companies to afford and leverage marketing automation.

Marketing automation provides a company with several key capabilities.

Understanding the Lead

Behavior tracking builds up a lead's profile. Most platforms provide tracking scripts and out-of-the-box behavior tracking of their assets (e.g., emails). This includes but is certainly not limited to email opens, email clicks, page views, form fills, social shares, and more. This provides data but no insight. When you combine the capability of advanced workflow automation with these behaviors and a company's products and/or value propositions, you can create custom logic to determine a lead's genuine interest.

Relevantly Engaging the Lead Omnichannel

With advanced workflow automation and the lead's genuine interest, you can make automated decisions to engage leads on topics they're interested in, on the channel they prefer, and at the exact right moment in their buyer journey. And as channels and tools evolve ever quicker, it's important to make sure your marketing automation platform is open by design and easily connectable.

"Seventy percent of buying experiences are based on how customers feel they're being understood."

McKinsey

57

Increasing Sales Productivity

The days of sales calling leads without context are over. Marketing automation provides the CRM with vital contextual data (e.g., interests, recent behavior, etc.). It also prioritizes leads to call based on quality, likeliness to buy, and urgency.

Marketing Insights

Marketing automation connects sales revenue to marketing efforts on the individual level, which allows companies to pinpoint which marketing investments drive revenue and which don't. This is vital to beat the competition.

Companies in the software market typically promote and sell their products in a specific way. They say their products are so easy, as if simply using their software magically solves all your challenges. But marketing automation is not a magical red button for success!

"Marketing automation is not a magical red button for success."

Marketing automation provides you with a toolbox to automate commercial processes, and it provides you with a platform to rapidly test and scale ideas that drive business revenue. But you can't drive more revenue without ideas and a solid commercial strategy. I'll explain more about that in the chapter called "When Marketing Automation Doesn't Work."

This Chapter's Challenges	This Chapter's Solutions
In this customer-centric age, our audiences expect us to be relevant, but how?	To be relevant, one must first understand. This is where marketing automation plays a vital role. Interpret behavior and engage accordingly.
How does marketing automation impact a company's competitive edge?	For most industries, marketing automation is already vital. Without it, a company would be crushed by its competitors within the next few years. For some industries, a company can still be an early adopter though.
Marketing automation is not a magical red button for success.	You need a solid commercial strategy, which you can combine with a platform that allows you to rapidly test and scale ideas that add business value.

HOW MARKETING AND SALES CAN ALIGN

It's the start of 2015. The start of my third year at Quintiq. We're closing in on hiring employee one thousand with our annual double digital growth. This is when I really start accelerating my growth in marketing automation. One of the biggest factors in becoming successful in marketing automation is how well you're able to align with sales. One of the other pillars is based around change management and making sure changes stick. How to make marketing and sales align is still one of the most-asked key questions in marketing automation. I've attended many keynotes in the past. And I will attend many more in the years to come. In March of 2015, I'm even copresenting a session on marketing and sales alignment with two other Marketo Engage users at the Marketing Nation Summit in San Francisco. No matter how long I search the internet, I haven't found a recipe for success. The only content that works for me is listening to others and reading about their successes. All these stories seem to build a picture in my mind of what could work in my situation. The notion of learning from the experiences of others also prompts me to share more. Next to my previous presentations about marketing automation at SiriusDecisions Summit and MarTech Conference, I want to share my "Road to Successful Marketing Automation" and "Journey to Successful Marketing Operations," a presentation about my three years at Quintiq. I start building my presentation, and in late 2015, I apply to speak at the next Marketing Nation Summit in Las Vegas in 2016. And a few years later, you're reading this book on the same topic but with a ten-year journey instead of a three-year time span.

"Success in marketing and sales alignment often comes in the accumulation of a lot of smaller successes."

People seem to be looking for the big epiphany in marketing and sales alignment. But success in marketing and sales alignment often comes in the accumulation of a lot of smaller successes (e.g., prospect portals).

At Quintiq, there wasn't too much collaboration between marketing and sales in the beginning. Most business units recruited marketers straight from school. Most of these juniors were too inexperienced compared to their veteran sales colleagues.

As a global marketing automation team and global sales operations team, we realize we're not only bridging business and IT. We are also bridging marketing and sales in the field. We sometimes organize cross–business unit meetings where people can learn from the best practices of others. We also actively look for best practices in the field and share these with others.

We also realize that we manage the entire buyer journey and sales process together, from awareness to winning the deal. Our MAP and their CRM are the left and right chambers of the heart of the commercial machine. We start doing everything together. Whenever offices must be relocated in the building, we make sure to have our rooms next to each other. And we even have our team outings together. Together, we align on every innovation. It was one of the most exhilarating periods in my career.

Other small successes in alignment come from how we enrich CRM. Sometimes senior sales members are really traditional and don't fully trust marketing yet. And they feel uncomfortable when marketing starts sending emails to their prospects. To gain their trust, we create a nurture overview in CRM. We create a field called "Active Nurture Program" on the person object in CRM (and MAP). The field is empty or populated with the current nurture program the person is in. We then create a report for sales and sales managers to view all their companies and see what percent of the contacts in it are being nurtured. When they expand, they can see which contacts are being nurtured and in which nurture program. This allows sales to decide to stop or start nurturing as they see fit.

"The way you communicate and introduce innovations is also vital to success in marketing and sales alignment."

The way you communicate is also vital to success. I often use an anecdote to explain this to people in discussions and my keynotes, as I see it happening so many times. So you might recognize yourself in the following scenario.

You want to introduce a new field for MAP, which you want in CRM. You want sales to populate a value in the new field. That way, you can enrich your data in MAP.

Maybe you want to start tracking "Disqualified Reason". You spend a lot of effort and money to generate new names. Some of them score enough points and become MQLs. These are sent to sales in CRM. Sales accepts them. Or sales disqualifies them. But you don't know why. You create a new field and start briefing sales. You provide them with work instructions and explain why you need the field. And you explain that they now need to spend even more time on administration—a recipe for rejection and failure! What would be a better way?

What's in It for Them (WIIFT)
But what if, during a workshop, you show sales that 50% of their opportunities are sourced from the MQLs you provide to them. You also show that 40% of the MQLs you provide are being disqualified. You ask them how much time it takes them to disqualify these MQLs. You then propose a solution. What if you no longer send them that bad 40%, only the great 60%? All the sales representatives are excited about the idea of reducing 40% of lead qualification. You ask them why they disqualify those leads. Together, you generate a list of reasons. And now you're ready to pitch your idea. You explain to them that you need to know which exact leads are disqualified for those reasons so you can track the root cause. Maybe these leads originate from certain campaigns or sources? You will share with them that you'll create a new field called "Disqualified Reason". For every lead they disqualify, they will have to pick a reason. This might be some extra administration for sales in the short term. But it will help you discover why leads get disqualified, so you can improve your scoring and logic, which will then result in sales spending less time on administration.

> *"Providing contextual data in CRM can help you in marketing and sales alignment early on."*

Another thing that can help you in sales alignment early on is providing contextual data in CRM. Whenever sales is looking at a person or company, they will see more than just a name, title, phone number, and/or industry. They'll see a much richer profile due to marketing's efforts. This allows them to better prepare qualifying calls, and it will increase the proportion of calls that lead to meetings.

Which Contextual Data Can You Share in CRM beyond Basic Properties?

Recent Engagement
When sales is about to call a prospect, they are looking for something to start the conversation. Any recent activity from the lead can be useful. You can provide sales with which key pages the lead visited. You can also list how they engaged with emails you sent and what forms they recently filled out on the website. Listing which nurture program(s) the lead was/is in can also provide context.

Important Downloads, Event Registrations, or Watched Videos
One of the key engagements is downloads. Downloading a whitepaper is often a display of heightened interest in that specific topic. Be aware of false positives though. I often see people boost open rates with great subject lines and titles without increasing click-through rates. Using clickbait can be tempting to generate new names, but the quality is low. Those people can also be disappointed when the content isn't what they expected. Then you generated a new name that starts off with a negative experience.

Especially for whitepapers, you don't want to measure only if people clicked through to the PDF. You want to make sure you track which pages are read (with a minimum seconds-per-page threshold). This is a much better insight than a click to a PDF. Tip: Implement a tracked PDF viewer.

Probable Topic(s) of Interest
You can list all the titles of all the pages and downloads, but instead of just providing this data, you want to show insight. You want to show what a lead is interested in. You're probably already using lead scoring to detect buying propensity and push those leads to sales. But you can also implement interest scoring. Make a new score field for every value proposition or value proposition category. Roughly apply the same concepts for lead scoring but limited to that specific value proposition category. You also apply score reduction for periods of inactivity. That way, you also know the category a lead is most interested in. Be sure to consider the importance of a good naming convention here.

Another way would be to list subscribing and unsubscribing to specific categories (in your preference center). Then sales doesn't have to engage the lead on a specific category that the lead has already unsubscribed from.

A very successful insight that I share with sales at Quintiq is "renewed interest," which is when the lead is inactive for a while but suddenly becomes active again. Active activity is preferable to latent activity, but you could use both. Imagine that sales is talking to a lead, and the lead says that they are not ready to buy now but maybe in twelve months. Sales asks if they can call back in twelve months. And sales marks their calendar to call back in eleven months. When they call back after eleven months, the lead tells them they are too late, as they just bought elsewhere two months ago. Looking at the data, you see that they started to visit the website again about four months ago, but they never called. With this lesson learned, you now create a workflow to inform sales of renewed interest after a period of inactivity. You can even create CRM tasks for sales to follow up on.

Urgency, Priority, and Propensity to Buy
You want to mention a lead's score, the propensity to buy. And you also want to show the relative score in stars and the urgency in flames as I described a few chapters earlier. This will allow sales to focus on their best bets first (those with more stars and flames). You don't want your hottest leads to cool down because sales didn't prioritize them.

Something else you can show—either directly or indirectly by integrating it into the lead's score—is intent. Several data providers have data on intent. I won't flood you with the names of these vendors, but they are out there. The simplest explanation is that they collect search data, which they cross-reference with reverse-IP lookups and other data. They are then able to say which companies are looking for certain products and/or services.

Surveys and/or Satisfaction
Customer feedback, or prospect feedback, is one of the most valuable insights you can get. In this age of customer centricity, we want to be relevant. We must first understand a person in order to be relevant to them. We typically use implicit data, such as digital behavior, to detect interest. But you can also ask for it explicitly through welcome surveys, questionnaires, customer satisfaction surveys, web polls, and other forms of feedback. Make sure this vital feedback is directly available for sales to tap into! I found it so important that I ended up presenting on it in several keynotes and videos throughout 2019 and 2020.

Campaign Membership

Campaign membership isn't as vital as the insights mentioned above, but it is something most marketers and sales do ask for. People want to know which campaigns the person engaged in. Were they an event attendee or webinar registrant? Unless the event had a very specific focus, it doesn't tell much about a lead's interest, but it can provide an easy conversation starter for sales.

Tip: Don't let sales wait till after an event is over to call registrants. That would be a missed opportunity. Call them right after they registered. Ask them why they registered. Ask them what they expect to gain from attending. Ask them if they already have certain questions they would love to see answered at the event. It will allow you to extend the experience way beyond the hours of the event. It will allow you to start addressing those key questions the buyer needs answers to.

What Else?

Of course, there is much more you could share with sales in CRM. Align with them but be critical. Distinguish data from information and information from insights. You want to avoid a situation where sales can no longer see the forest for the trees. Don't overwhelm them. It will lower the value. Choose wisely to make an impact.

Work together with sales on the exact details and format of the contextual data. Explain what you can and can't provide. Prioritize what sales finds important. Plan recurring meetings to keep discussing and improving the contextual data. It's a great opener to discuss other ways you can help sales. An additional benefit is that being heard increases trust.

Take that physical alignment a step further. Lay a foundation of structural alignment. Maybe you can introduce biweekly marketing-sales meetings or quarterly business reviews (QBRs). Just don't use a loose format for these meetings, as you will risk low attendance.

An Example Agenda for a Biweekly Marketing-Sales Meeting

Make sure you have leadership involvement. Preferably, you will have already discussed the reports and KPIs with the director the day before the meeting. That way, you and the director can already make up your minds as to what the next best actions would be. If you don't, there is a real chance the director will be surprised by some metrics and try to "defend" their marketers and sales' performance. They might even dismiss the metrics as untrustworthy.

- Last period
  - o Completed events/campaigns
  - o KPI trends
    - ▪ New names generated
    - ▪ MQLs
    - ▪ MQL>SAL ratio and disqualification
    - ▪ Call-to-meeting ratio
    - ▪ Mutation on opportunity pipeline
    - ▪ Closed won deals
    - ▪ Lost deals
  - o Open reflection on what went well and what did not
- Next period
  - o Upcoming events/campaigns
    - ▪ E.g., action list
  - o What to do to turn around negative KPI trendlines
  - o Other commercial initiatives

The example above is by no means a best-practice agenda. The main idea is that you inform each other of what you are doing. Because, together, you try to create demand and sell. Second, you reflect and tell each other what can be improved. And you establish what lessons you have learned.

Tip: During your quarterly business reviews, open two or three of the key opportunities that you closed that quarter. Look at all the engagement with the persons in the account from first contact up to opportunity creation and closing the opportunity (Marketo Engage users can use the Opportunity Influence Analyzer for this). After a while, these qualitative discussions will result in insights into what works well and what doesn't during the different stages of the sales process.

Structurally aligning marketing and sales is the first step toward achieving account-based marketing (ABM). ABM is flaming hot in 2015. And it still is in 2020 when I'm writing this paragraph. But ABM is as old as sales. It's nothing new. Marketing is there to eventually sell your products and services. In the past, marketers were not able to sufficiently prove how they directly contributed to sales. Technology simply made this possible.

There are three types of markets you can be active in, according to SiriusDecisions.

An Existing Solution for an Existing Challenge

You might offer financial bookkeeping services. These are existing services for an existing challenge. Every company has to report on financial results. These markets are mature. Companies already have a budget for these types of services. And you often find yourself competing on price. You can avoid this somewhat by providing exceptional customer experience and/or value-added services. As a marketer, you don't have to convince your prospect they have a challenge. They know! And you don't have to convince them of your solution. They know!

A Better Solution for an Existing Challenge

You might have invented a completely new way of dealing with a challenge. One example is offering electric-powered vehicles instead of gasoline-powered vehicles—a better solution for an existing transportation challenge. The transportation market is an established and mature market where companies often compete on price. Your new and better solution is likely more expensive. As a marketer, you will have to convince people why your solution is better and why they should pay more for your solution. Your prospects likely haven't budgeted for those extra investments.

A New Solution for a New Challenge

You're dealing with long and complex buyer journeys when you have a solution for a challenge nobody knows they have. You'll first have to educate people and make them aware they even have a challenge. Only then will you be able to sell them your solution for it. And they will not have any budget reserved for it.

The market you're active in defines the focus of your marketing efforts. But in B2B, it usually comes down to informing sales which leads have the highest propensity to buy right now so that the expensive sales force can focus on where they do best. Some companies have very defined target markets. They might have already identified the eighty companies that could buy their solutions. As a marketer, you would still help in the same way. You help identify new names at those target accounts, and you prioritize those with the highest propensity to buy.

The biggest challenge is that sales seems obsessed with a focus on the companies, while marketing has a focus on people in companies. Don't blame sales for this. They want to wheel in a company, and they don't have any names of people yet. No wonder they have a company focus instead of a people focus. But people do business with people. Financial entities do not magically buy from each other without human interaction. Well, at least to my knowledge.

Be sales' partner and help them discover new decision makers. You could use prospect portals for this. But when talking about target companies where you don't have an opportunity yet, you can use account portals. I launched the first account portal about ten months after the first prospect portal was launched at Quintiq.

Account Portals

Account portals work well for when your target accounts have a specific industry challenge you can address with your solution. Rather than sending people from the company to your generic website to search for relevant content, you create a landing page where you mention the exact content you have that might answer their  key questions. You can also describe their likely challenges to display that you understand their needs. You can already introduce real people they would likely engage with when contacting you.

In 2015, my team at Quintiq expands its scope well beyond marketing automation. In addition to technology, we are also covering marketing training, education, onboarding, processes, analytics, dashboards, and insights (e.g., we prepare insights for marketing-sales meetings). So we rename ourselves to the marketing operations team. But what are the ingredients for success?

This Chapter's Challenges	This Chapter's Solutions
What's the big secret in aligning marketing and sales?	It's not a big thing. It's an accumulation of smaller successes.
Which role can a corporate MOps and SOps team play in alignment?	MOps and Sops should be tightly aligned for marketing and sales to align too.
How to gain sales' trust to let marketing send emails to their prospects and customers?	Provide sales with a (real-time) report/view into which of their contacts and accounts are being nurtured in which program. Provide a brochure with each nurture program. This allows sales to read about what happens during such a nurture program.
How to find support in introducing innovations and changes to CRM and MAP? How to avoid objections to change?	The ways marketing and sales communicate, collaborate, and involve each other to introduce innovations are vital for success in their alignment.
Don't know where to start? What is a quick win for marketing and sales alignment?	Providing contextual data in CRM helps marketing and sales alignment early on.

How to avoid false positives when trying to understand a lead's interest?	Don't simply track page views. Adjust your scoring scripts to include page size and seconds on the page. This provides a weight to the page view. Apply the same for PDFs. Don't only register the click to a PDF. Track every PDF page that is viewed for a minimum number of seconds.
If lead score is for buying propensity in general, with multiple value propositions, how to know in which proposition a lead is genuinely interested?	Create an interest scoring field per value proposition (or value proposition category) and a matching scoring program. Much like lead scoring, but limited to the specific value proposition (e.g., specific web pages, keywords used, etc.).
Are there formats available to get momentum in aligning marketing and sales?	Biweekly marketing and sales meetings or quarterly business reviews (QBR).
Are there specific requirements for ABM related to marketing and sales alignment?	Success in account-based marketing (ABM) requires structurally aligning marketing and sales first.
What can marketing do before handing over leads to sales? What are typical examples?	How marketing can collaborate with sales also depends on which of the three core markets you are active in: existing solutions for an existing challenge, a new and better solution for an existing challenge, or new solutions for a new challenge.

What is an easy first step in leveraging technology for account-based marketing?

You start with strategy and technology follows! Not the other way around. Too many companies buy an ABM solution, thinking it will allow them to magically be good at ABM. It starts with aligning with sales on which accounts to target and how. A simple tool, however, could be to leverage account portals.

HOW TO BECOME A MARKETING AUTOMATION CHAMPION?

Throughout the journey in this book, I'm sharing knowledge and experience in the same order as I gained it over ten years, switching between the client side and agency side multiple times. Later, I founded my own agency. The experience I gained is not only about the technology and the business processes themselves. I also grew as a professional and on a personal level, giving me even more lessons I can share.

I often got questions about how to become and be seen as a marketing automation champion. People want to get tips on how to progress in their careers or how to start and grow their marketing agency. This is always a blend between knowledge, experience, and ways to leverage those to make an impact on a company. Making an impact on a company requires change. And change is difficult. Unfortunately, there is no easy button to digital success. Change doesn't come overnight; it takes a multiyear investment. Many people look for shortcuts. But like Jeff Coveney, another MarTech fanatic I have known for many years, said, "Many companies want the results and reports with shortcuts. It's kind of like wanting to compete in a triathlon without the training."

> "Many companies want the results and reports with shortcuts. It's kind of like wanting to compete in a triathlon without the training."
>
> *Jeff Coveney*

Before joining Quintiq in late 2012, I already kept a blog to share as much as I could to help others succeed. There wasn't much left to learn for me regarding theory. But I had plenty left to learn and experience in practice. Before Quintiq, I had superficial experience with multiple marketing automation platforms. But at Quintiq, I started working with Marketo Engage and Salesforce daily. I even took over as leader of the Dutch Marketo Engage user group around January 2013.

I learned about the different advocate programs Marketo Engage set up. One of them was the Marketo Champion© initiative. I looked at the list of 2013 Champions and noticed a whole bunch of interesting people who I would love to meet, people from whom I could still learn a lot! I looked at the challenging criteria and realized I was already meeting a lot of them. I thought it should be feasible for me to become a Marketo Champion within one or two years.

At Marketo Summit in San Francisco in 2013, Marketo Engage introduced certification. I was in the first group of people to certify at the summit. Certification also became a requirement for becoming a Champion. I was thrilled when the 2014 class was announced with my name on the list. I made it to the worldwide top fifty elite class. This would add a lot of momentum to my career's trajectory.

I started to look at how I could leverage my Champion status and other Marketo Engage advocate programs to boost my career. And the great part about it? I could boost my career by doing what I love most—helping others succeed! But to help more people, I would need a bigger platform.

I didn't like to write, and I considered myself a poor writer. Though somehow I did commit to writing this book by myself. I have always chosen speaking, webcast, and/or video over blog posts and writing. If you like this book, please do let me and others know. Maybe I'll consider writing more often.

Keynotes on marketing automation, content marketing, and the like that I had seen so far were always superficial, mostly strategic or theoretical. Most presenters would talk about personas, DMUs, and journeys. Then they would skip a whole lot and maybe talk about the theory of scoring and nurturing. Nobody—and I mean nobody—ever showed how to actually do it. I think, next to my experience at Milestone, this is where my reservations about consultants came from. It seemed as if they didn't share and kept their cards close to their chest. So I came up with my first presentation outline in 2014. Ten how-tos for marketing automation. I titled it: "Optimize (with) Marketing Automation." I started with a five-to-ten-minute recap of all the theory they always hear from others. Then I created a bridge to the ten how-tos. The bridge was that orchestration of the complex omnichannel engagement can no longer be done manually. Automation is inevitable.

I then showed a buyer's journey and pinpointed ten likely challenges you have to overcome in real life. And I then went through each of these ten challenges in more detail. I could show people screenshots of how I solved them. These examples included: How to detect a lead's buyer journey stage? How to determine a lead's persona? How to know a lead's key questions? How to assign a lead to the best-matching nurture program? How to assign an MQL to the correct sales representative? How to attribute marketing success to a marketing campaign? My very first presentation was at Platform Innovation Marketing (PIM) in 2014.

> *"Orchestration of the complex omnichannel engagement can no longer be done manually. Automation is inevitable."*

My biggest challenge for that presentation was to fit everything I wanted to share into just thirty minutes. Impossible! Looking back at that first presentation, I had so much to learn about presenting. Even when looking back at my most recent presentation, I still think I have a lot more to learn. But I think it's a good thing to never stop improving. I also realized that it's okay to (still) be nervous when I have to present. And most important? I know I'm sharing knowledge that people can leverage. So I am reaching my goals.

I got the chance to redo that specific presentation a few more times at different venues in the months after PIM (e.g., SiriusDecisions Summit 2015). I also started thinking about a second storyline. A Ted-style talk, which I first presented at MarTech Conference in 2015. The title? "The Road to Successful Marketing Operations." Sound familiar? The slides had a visual timeline at the bottom. It covered the highlights of my two and a half years at Quintiq. The same two and a half years are also included in this book's ten-year journey.

My different speaking opportunities also resulted in many interviews with blogs and magazines, which, in turn, resulted in additional speaking opportunities. I learned that they strengthened each other. The more momentum your thought leadership has, the more traction there is. If one element slows down, so does everything else.

I enjoyed being able to help others with my experience. Still not fond of writing at the time, I searched for more ways to help others. I started meeting with marketing leaders from different companies. I reserved about one hour every week in my schedule to discuss digital marketing and marketing automation with others. It was a nice way to mix things up. It allowed me to not get stuck in a bubble at Quintiq. You don't know what you don't know. I got the chance to discuss the digital challenges and successes of other companies. The marketing leaders of those companies were happy to be able to talk to an independent expert for free. I learned that people like myself in the software space were much more experienced than people in other markets, such as manufacturing.

My drive to keep helping others resulted in being renamed Marketo Champion© in 2015 and 2016. In those years, about ten out of the fifty Champions were new each year. I was now among a small group of multi-champions. In 2019, when the program was revamped, I was named Marketo Champion Alumni. But in 2020 and 2021, I was renamed to active Champion yet again.

As a result of my Marketo Engage honors, my LinkedIn inbox exploded with job offers. But I felt so at home at Quintiq. I wasn't planning on going anywhere else soon. There was still so much to innovate and grow at Quintiq. Not only did I receive job offers on LinkedIn, but I also received more questions from people. Some people had very specific questions on Marketo Engage, but others wanted to know where to start or how to leverage the value of marketing automation.

> *"Your marketing automation platform should enable you to drive business value through rapidly testing, running, and scaling commercial improvements. It digitally transforms you."*

I was looking for a way to list the requirements to achieve success with marketing automation. I did not see one successful campaign as an indication of success with marketing automation. Marketing automation is so much more than campaigning. Your marketing automation platform should enable you to drive business value through rapidly testing, running, and scaling commercial improvements. It digitally transforms you.

My first requirements were based around people, process, and technology. My second iteration focused on campaigns, operations, and insights. But in 2020, I was inspired by a short article that a colleague at Chapman Bright found in the Harvard Business Review, called, "Digital Transformation Comes Down to Talent in 4 Key Areas." The article described different needs for technology, data, process, and change management.

Digital Transformation Comes Down to Talent in Four Key Areas

Since that article, I have switched from my initial three angles to four quadrants when talking about marketing technology. The figures below are examples that we used in MarTech transformation projects at Chapman Bright.

Technology	Data
• In a decentralized organization, a strong central technological backbone needs to offer local flexibility to execute. • As market needs and technological developments move fast, an agile change process needs to be in place. • A well integrated CRM-MAP team is a powerful core for any digital commercial stack.	• In order to provide a personalized customer experience, full visibility on customer data (demographics and behaviour) is crucial. • In order to continuously learn and improve, one needs to define assumptions and measure results against them. • Data needs to be handled with the utmost respect, always complying with regulations and customer expectations.
• Clarity on the digital roadmap, processes to add / change items on it and decision-making process will improve buy-in. • Providing easily consumable training materials for key processes helps develop the internal skills level. • A knowledge portal with appealing and up to date content and an actively maintained interactive component improves team involvement. **Process**	• A clear vision and explicit benefits that follow from it are crucial for team commitment. • Making progress and benefits visible as they materialize stimulates momentum. • People need to be able to join the change process at their own terms and speed. • Breaking the journey down into smaller pieces and tackling those one by one ensures consistent progress towards the end goal. **Change Management**

Technology	Data
• Understanding required technological capabilities • Deciding what needs to be built, bought or outsourced • Selecting tools that meet company specific needs • Integrate in a joined-up model • Accessible to local users	• 360-degree view on customer data • Data management & protection processes that respect (local) regulations • In-house visibility • Defining KPI's that underpin creation of business value
• Clearly defined workflows, roles and responsibilities • Documented best practices / tips & tricks • Training materials and program to ensure skills levels • Company-wide knowledge sharing via standardized exchange methods • Agile and clearly documented change request processes **Process**	• One clearly defined identity & vision • One or more senior executives visibly championing both identity and vision • An established company culture of continuous improvement • Stimulating new ideas • Openness to fail and learn **Change Management**

Technology

The potential of emerging technologies is immense. Scott Brinker's MarTech landscape showed us the increase of available technologies. And they have become much easier to use. But a lot of companies have legacy technology environments that are holding them back. Thinking beyond these current limitations, IT's alignment with the business, and being allowed to fail and experiment are all vital to success.

Data

Companies are gathering more and more data. Data that is often never even used. And most companies realize their data quality is poor. How can you engage your audience relevantly if you don't understand them (based on their data)? So why do so few companies budget for data quality? Though we must not forget engaging with a humanistic purpose, we do have to become better at data-driven decisions.

Process

Transformation is not the same as change. People need to start thinking beyond silos and hierarchical structures. Not only should you improve current processes in the direction of customers, but you should also design completely new processes when required.

Change Management

Data, technology, and process are all very exact. But people are crucial. Companies need people with the right mindset and capability to change. A lot of transformations do not reach their goals because companies overlook the people aspect.

The original HBR article that inspired me to further improve my marketing technology success model can be read on:

https://hbr.org/2020/05/digital-transformation-comes-down-to-talent-in-4-key-areas.

HBR.org

Throughout 2015, I started to do more and more presentations. And it wasn't long before people in the audience started to ask if I could consult for them on marketing automation. Would I be open to start freelancing?

That question was not new to me. I had asked myself that question many years earlier when I was an online marketer. Back then, I was focused on search engine optimization (SEO), for example. And back then, I said no. I figured that I only had a few years of working experience. And I foresaw that online marketing could easily be commoditized. Skills like search engine optimization or managing Google Adwords campaigns are relatively easy to develop. As a result, more and more companies could employ and train people straight out of school, and hourly rates for this work would drop.

But I realized that consulting on marketing technology was not something that could easily be commoditized. However, I did have a few other concerns. A lot of people saw me as a genuine independent thought leader, as I worked on the client side. Would that still be the case as a consultant? Would I still be invited as a speaker? Would people still trust that I'm truly there to help them succeed, or would they merely think I was there to sell my services?

However, as a consultant, I would be able to help even more people than through just speaking. I wouldn't just inspire them; I would be able to help them. At the time, I still had reservations about consulting. But this wasn't my biggest concern.

My wife worked part-time, and most of my family's income was dependent on my salary at Quintiq. Silvy, Suze, Iza, and I had just moved into the new house two years before. So we didn't have much of a financial reserve. Leaving Quintiq, a company where there still was a lot for me to do, was something that took some months of consideration. What should I do?

This Chapter's Challenges	This Chapter's Solutions
Many companies want the results and reports with shortcuts. It's kind of like wanting to compete in a triathlon without the training.	There is no magic button for quick success. You must constantly test ideas and scale those that work.
How to cross the barrier between theory and practice in marketing automation?	Realizing that orchestration of the complex omnichannel engagement can no longer be done manually. Automation is inevitable.
How to advance my thought leadership and/or career in marketing automation?	Advocate programs of MarTech suppliers can be great to boost your career.
How to turn your expertise into thought leadership?	Speaking opportunities, interviews, blogs, and expert meetings create synergy. They strengthen each other and create momentum for your thought leadership journey. If you're not speaking yet, simply apply when events have a "call for speakers."
It's okay to be nervous when presenting.	Remember that you're trying to help others succeed by sharing your experiences.
Which factors influence the chances of success with marketing automation?	Realize your MarTech transformation by keeping four quadrants in mind: technology, data, process, and change management.

HOW TO ACHIEVE AWARD-WORTHY ROI

It's still 2015, and the team and I at Quintiq make further improvements to our nurture campaigns. We're also making steps toward better understanding and measuring its contribution to the business. In our initial findings, we noticed that our improvements to the nurture campaigns resulted in three times more revenue attribution. Further analysis supports these findings (e.g., higher click-through rates of the nurture emails).

We submit the details on our nurture strategy, the campaign architecture, and the results to an awards committee in the United States. We look at the winners of previous years and realize that simply being nominated would already be an honor. We'll even be happy with some great feedback. It comes as a total surprise to learn Quintiq won the Killer Content Award for best nurture strategy. Other winners and nominees in other categories include IBM, Glassdoor, and Marketo.

The combination of being named twice to the Champion Top50 and the Killer Content Award resulted in yet more speaking opportunities for me—a bigger stage to share my knowledge and experience to help others succeed.

News travels fast, even at Quintiq internally. In my view, it allows me to talk to colleagues higher up in the hierarchy. The reasoning behind that is that I now feel more confident that I'm doing the right things. My team is now more involved with the marketers of all twelve business units around the world. It allows me to focus on their business unit directors. With the CMO leaving the company for a new adventure, I'm working with the CEO to calculate next year's targets for marketing. I'm a bit nervous because he's a mathematician. But I realize this just provides me with a fresh pair of eyes to help me choose better targets.

It was quite a journey to get to this point, calculating marketing's targets. To set a target, you must also be able to measure it. And to measure something, you must have a sense of the metric. And then you need to generate the data for that metric. And you need to put processes in place to ensure you'll get that data. I had taken a few turns in my journey to get to that point where I was in mid-2015.

My first attempt at visualizing marketing's contribution at Quintiq was in late 2013. I've always been an exact sciences type of guy. So I was excited when I got introduced to marketing attribution models. I immediately tried to launch the models that Marketo Engage introduced. However, it's important to know that all companies are different. How do you market? How do you sell? How long is your buyer's journey? Which one will best fit Quintiq?

First Touch Attribution (FT)

The main driver behind attribution is connecting marketing efforts to revenue. A first touch could be if a previously unknown person at a company that you're not yet engaging with fills out a marketing form on your website, and later on, that company signs a deal with you. You can then attribute the total value of that deal to the marketing initiative that made the person fill out the form.

As a result, some deals will be sourced by marketing and some not (e.g., sales sourced). Reality is much more complex, however. In business-to-business deals, there are typically multiple people involved in the buying journey. So multiple contacts are associated with an opportunity. Some of these contacts can have a first touch by marketing while the other contacts don't. How will I attribute the first touch?

Most platforms will divide the opportunity value equally over the number of contacts associated with it and then attribute those that have a marketing first touch. One problem with this is that the resulting values no longer make sense to sales. They simply don't match their pipeline values. It disconnects marketing from sales instead of connecting them.

Another thing to consider is which opportunity value I'll be using. The opportunity amount, for example. But is the opportunity amount updated with the exact amount of the signed contract at some point? Will I be looking at only open pipeline, closed pipeline, or total pipeline? So will I look at first touch revenue or first touch created pipeline? Only looking at won deals seems like the most appealing to me as an exact sciences guy. But Quintiq has long sales cycles, nine to eighteen months on average. In some new upcoming regions, it's even longer. If I want to move toward data-driven decisions, I can't work with metrics that are eighteen months old.

So if sales cycles are long, it might be better to opt for First Touch created pipeline. But there are more challenges. It all depends on sales properly assigning opportunity roles for contacts. If a contact is not technically associated with an opportunity, there is no way to give the contact credit for the opportunity value. Fortunately, Quintiq does set contact roles for opportunities! As any respectable company in B2B should.

"It's absolutely critical that sales in B2B works the entire decision-making unit (DMU) to get the deal. If sales is not even able to indicate who's in the DMU in CRM, the chance of them wining the deal drops proportionally."

Though some companies fail to properly manage this. Some platforms, like Marketo Engage and Bizible, allow you to change settings. You can switch between exact, indirect, or hybrid attribution. With indirect, it will give credit to any contact in the company, regardless of whether the contact is associated with the opportunity or not. This seems like a solution, but it is not. A company might have dozens or hundreds of contacts listed in CRM, and many might have absolutely nothing to do with the opportunity.

The biggest challenge comes from how sales adds contacts to the CRM. Or how they process and convert your leads to contacts. The most common scenario I see is one where marketing generates a lead. The lead is passed on to inside sales. They call the lead. The lead says she's researching suppliers for her manager. Inside sales asks for her manager's information. Inside sales creates a new contact in CRM for that manager and passes it on to sales for a meeting. Any opportunity that is only connected to the new contact might look like sales sourced, but it was actually marketing sourced. The original lead must also be converted as a contact to that same account. And that converted lead must then also be given a role in the opportunity. That will be the difference between the opportunity being recognized as sourced by sales or marketing.

First Touch attribution also has many different variations. Do I consider the first "touch" the first touch? For example, the display ad someone clicked. (First Touch Attribution). Or do I consider the moment the person became known as a lead to be the first touch? (Lead Creation Touch Attribution).

There are also variations directed toward the last touch. This could be at the moment the opportunity is created (Opportunity Creation Touch Attribution) or the last touch just before the opportunity is created (Last Nondirect Touch Attribution), which can be further drilled down to Last Channel Touch Attribution.

Multitouch Attribution (MT)

While all the first touch models give credit for sourcing revenue, they don't value marketing efforts that occur once the lead has become known up until they sign a deal with you. I'm especially enthusiastic about the multitouch model in Marketo Engage. Every marketing effort is captured in a program in Marketo Engage. People become a member of a campaign (e.g., invited to or attended a webinar). And I can define what I consider success (e.g., registered for and/or attended an event) for each channel/type. All the people with a role in an opportunity will be assigned a share of the opportunity value. And that value will then be distributed over all the campaigns where the people had success. Some people have success in the same campaigns of course. Eventually, this provides a monetary attribution value for all campaigns. This is called linear attribution. It's the simplest way of calculating multitouch attribution. One problem is that on top of equally valuing each contact, it also equally values each campaign with the same weight in its contribution to the revenue. One way to address that is to use time decay attribution. It shifts more value to campaigns closer to the deal. This seems fairer but will make top-of-funnel efforts look like they are less effective.

More difficult to implement are U-shaped, W-shaped, and Z-shaped models that give more credit to specific touch points (e.g., how the lead first entered the door, how they became known, and how the opportunity got created).

More attribution
models

84

Calculating ROI

A benefit of dividing revenues over marketing campaigns is that they can be combined with the costs of that marketing campaign. There will be campaigns that get attributed a lot of revenue but also cost more. I can get an ROI percentage by dividing the revenue attribution by the associated cost. That way, I can see which marketing effort has the highest ROI. This can help the marketers at Quintiq make better investment decisions and make better plans and budgets for the next year. I start to manually add costs to campaigns. This is easy for events and other out-of-pocket spending. But a lot of marketing's efforts have no out-of-pocket costs. And some campaigns take a lot of time, while others don't. Some of my fellow Marketo Champions add arbitrary costs for hours spent on campaigns. That comes with two challenges. The first is getting marketers to keep time sheets. That will not be a popular decision. The second challenge is determining an appropriate hourly rate. It will require me to know how much each employee costs per hour. Otherwise, it would be hard to balance actual out-of-pocket costs with fictive hourly costs.

Calculating ROI seems too farfetched at this moment, especially because I'm having a hard time getting people on board with even the generic FT and MT models in Marketo Engage that I'm endorsing. Even my explainer videos don't seem to turn the tide. Sales, in particular, can't correlate these attribution numbers to the numbers they normally discuss, which are pipeline and revenue in Euros. And sales is not interested in learning who sourced an opportunity. They don't care if marketing or sales sourced it. They are the ones closing all the deals anyway.

"Great metrics are not great if they divide marketing and sales instead of aligning them."

Great metrics are not great if they divide marketing and sales instead of aligning them. If I want sales and marketing to come together for a common goal, they must both fully comprehend each other's metrics and language. We at marketing should stop inventing things ourselves and stop complaining that we can't get sales on board with these new inventions. We should sit together and come up with something together!

Back to the drawing board. Let's start with unveiling what we truly want to achieve. The first breakthrough is that everybody confirms where new business opportunities come from. Sales sources new business on their own (e.g., from their network or chasing strategic accounts). Or they get hot prospects from inside sales. Inside sales gets their prospects on their own (e.g., from their network or chasing named accounts). Or they get qualified leads from marketing.

The biggest discussions come from deciding when something is marketing sourced or sales sourced. When do we attribute revenue? What if a former sales representative added a contact to the CRM many years ago, but a marketer emailed that person and convinced them to attend an event. The contact attends the event and then signs a deal three months later. Or what if marketing generated a lot of new names with an event many years ago. One of those names is dormant for a while. Then sales calls this person, and three months later, a deal is signed. Is it marketing sourced or sales sourced? More importantly, whatever the original source, what feels fair and just to all of us?

A decision is made. If there's a marketing success with an opportunity-associated contact in the twelve months before that opportunity's creation, the opportunity is marketing sourced. Unless there was a sales success in the three months before that first marketing success.

What is a marketing success? And what is a sales success? We review all our campaigns and channels. Which progression statuses do we consider successes (e.g., webinar registration and/or attendance)? With very limited adjustments, we're tracking marketing success. And we even have historic data. Thank you, marketing automation.

We're in a lucky position where sales is also logging their calls and meetings in CRM. This is part of a sales effectiveness program that the sales operations team is running with the CEO. There's a big incentive on properly logging these. This enables us to easily ensure sales successes can also be measured. Any meetings that take place or calls with specific call outcomes are considered sales successes.

The next step is to gather, process, and then visualize the data for everybody. First, we have to know whether an opportunity is marketing or sales sourced according to our interpretation of first touch. Both sales and marketing can look at a single opportunity and see whether it's considered marketing sourced or sales sourced, regardless of whether appropriate roles are applied or the original source of the contact. We can then also see which percentage of opportunities, in a certain timeframe, are marketing sourced versus sales sourced.

KPIs

The Quality Management Team at Quintiq has several responsibilities. One of them is maintaining a periodic scorecard that lists all the business units per discipline (e.g., delivery, sales, legal, human resources, etc.). For each discipline, a business unit can get a score between zero and two hundred, where one hundred represents achieving the target. Each discipline weights the level of strategic importance in the eyes of leadership. The business unit's total score is used to adjust the bonus that employees of that business unit get. Second, no business unit wants to be the worst-performing business unit.

Prashant Gupta from the Quality Management Team helps me to add marketing to the company-wide scorecard. They already have access to a lot of systems to pull in the required data. The score for marketing will be based on three core elements:

- % of opportunities sourced by marketing
- € in marketing sourced pipeline
- # of leads turned to marketing-qualified leads (MQL)

Depending on the age of the business unit, the number of marketers, and the height of the marketing budget, the target percentage for marketing sourced opportunities is determined. The initial average target is about 30%. This then relates to a score of one hundred. More than 50% is capped at a score of two hundred. The second metric is easy to determine: 30% of the total sales pipeline target. All three scores are recalculated each week per business unit.

Knowing which opportunity is marketing sourced or sales sourced according to our logic, we can also further investigate marketing's performance.

Too often I hear people make a statement similar to:
"We generated ten thousand new names in 2015. Four thousand of those were marked as qualified and were sent to sales. One thousand of those four thousand became an opportunity. And five hundred of those one thousand turned into a deal in 2015."

Depending on the length of the average buyer's journey, some of the six thousand remaining new names from 2015 might become MQLs in 2016. And maybe some of the remaining three thousand MQLs might also turn into opportunities in 2016?

Most people somehow feel like they should compress metrics into calendar years, but reality doesn't care about artificial time frames. A buyer's journey transcends your arbitrary reporting timeframes. When you look at how many MQLs became opportunities in a certain time bucket, you should not limit that to only MQLs that also became MQLs in the same time bucket. When they became an MQL is irrelevant. The same applies to when generated leads become MQLs in a time bucket. You should be looking at any lead that became an MQL this quarter, regardless of when the lead was generated. I call this velocity reporting.

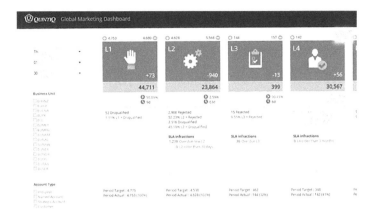

I really like SiriusDecision's Demand Waterfall. But even though Quintiq is a SiriusDecisions customer, we do not properly name our stages. We use L1 for inquiries, L2 for automated qualified leads, L3 for MQLs, L4 for sales accepted leads, L5 for opportunities, and L6 for won deals. And this is quite confusing because you might confuse those names for lead levels, which are something quite different.

The manager from our internal Online Marketing Team in Kuala Lumpur is helping me to develop a velocity dashboard for marketing. I create an instructional video for everybody at Quintiq on how to work with velocity metrics. You select a reporting time frame on the top left. For that reporting time frame, you can see (in the figure above) that 144 records turned into an L3 (MQL). And 157 turned from L3 into something else. So within the reporting time frame, the number of L3 in stock dropped by 13 and is now at 399.

If any stock is depleting over time, you'll already know in advance that you will run into future issues. It enables you to act before you get into trouble. Next to monitoring the mutations in stock, you can also see the conversion rates from each specific stage to the next stage, as well as how long it takes in days (or hours). Targets are established on internal averages as well as market benchmarks. This enables us to indicate in red or green whether the metric is healthy or not.

We then start adding all kinds of filters on the left to enable colleagues to drill down (e.g., by business unit, region, account types, etc.). For every filter we add, we first ensure 100% data quality for that field. This means the field must be populated in 100% of the cases. And there should be a documented process for how the field gets populated.

I've now covered the more strategic ways how we look at marketing's contribution at Quintiq. But we should also have better ways to make data-driven marketing decisions, which are less strategic. People often mix up a lot of KPIs and metrics. They often assess marketing initiatives on metrics whose hierarchy they do not understand. I see metrics in four different levels.

The Different Levels of Metrics

Numbers

The number of emails that you send. The number of respondents. The size of your audience. These are just numbers. These can support you in assessing whether you can reach your goal. Or they can provide you with some context when you try to troubleshoot issues in performance.

Conversion Level Metrics

Most marketers, often junior ones, seem obsessed with conversion level metrics. They do not tell you anything about whether the campaign created value and/or contributed to the business. These metrics provide you with insight on sub conversions, which can provide insights on how to further improve campaigns themselves (e.g., number of event registrations or percentage of registrations to attendance).

Campaign Level Metrics

I think these are the most interesting metrics. They tell you something about whether your campaign contributed to why you started it in the first place. Did you organize that event for driving new names or meetings for sales?

Strategic Level Metrics

These we already covered earlier this chapter (e.g., sourced pipeline). But all the metrics, regardless of their level, don't mean anything without the ability to put them into perspective. You need a benchmark. My marketing operations department also partly acts as a global demand center. We also build campaigns for business units. But there's more demand for our services than we can handle. I introduce campaign intake sheets in Microsoft Excel. A marketer must provide Excel spreadsheets with the campaign briefing. It allows us to assess the likely success of the campaign. We can then not only help the marketers with improvements and have more realistic expectations but also prioritize which campaigns deserve our time and resources.

A marketer should set their expected targets for up to twelve metrics for their campaign. The metrics depend on the channel and/or type of campaign, with up to three metrics for each of the four levels. To guide them toward a realistic number, market averages and Quintiq's averages are prefilled. Sometime after the campaign is finished, we add the actual results that were achieved. This allows the business to fully assess what happened and possibly drill down and learn to become better in the future.

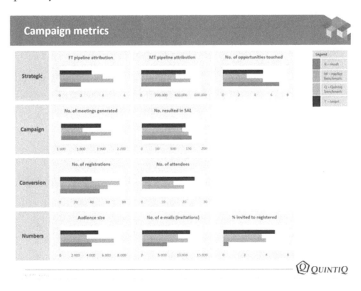

This Chapter's Challenges	This Chapter's Solutions
How to depict marketing's contribution to the business?	Business is often expressed as revenue. Revenue attribution models attribute a part of the pipeline toward marketing successes.
What kinds of revenue attribution models exist?	There are first touch and multitouch attribution models. Each has different variations and interpretations.
Which attribution model is the best for Quintiq?	Quintiq required a custom algorithm, due to its interpretation of marketing and sales successes over time.
How can we better understand and make data-driven decisions based on how leads progress through the marketing and sales process?	Velocity reporting enables you to determine how well leads progress in a certain time frame without limiting the source data to that same time frame.
Can metrics be categorized to better determine the impact of the success and contribution of campaigns?	Metrics can be put in four levels of hierarchy: numbers, conversion, campaign, and strategic. Higher levels tell something about the campaign's contribution to the business goals. The lower levels provide insights into how and where campaign improvements are possible.

HOW TO HELP OTHERS SUCCEED

At Quintiq, I learned that we, as the marketing operations team, were able to help colleagues succeed with our MarTech stack. Helping others succeed is one of the core elements in marketing operations. Loosely based on an older SiriusDecisions definition, I have used the following definition to describe marketing operations in many of my keynotes.

> "Marketing Operations (MOps) plays a crucial role in aligning strategy and processes throughout the organization to ensure that they are able to excel in their marketing efforts. Whether leveraging technology, creating processes, productizing best-practices, coordinating functions, training, reporting on performance, or generating new insights, Marketing Operations is at the center of much of the marketing organization's activity."

Diederik Martens

In May 2015, I present at a summit organized by SiriusDecisions. I share my ten tips on how to get things done with marketing automation. In the audience are marketers from Trend Micro. I already know them from the Dutch Marketo User Group. Inspired by the different presentations at the summit, they realize they need regional marketing operations as a discipline at Trend Micro. They confront me and share their ideas. They ask me if I would be open to supporting them as a contracted consultant. I still have my reservations about consulting, but I realize I would be able to genuinely help them improve. We have more discussions in the weeks after the summit to define more of the details about the role. We agree on a period of three months for about two to three days per week and an option to continue for a second quarter. It's a difficult decision for Silvy and me. Our new house drained our financial reserves, and most of our family's income comes from my job. But the contracted volume of this launching customer provides me with enough security to quit my job at Quintiq.

I go to the Chamber of Commerce to register my company. I already know the name. Rob from Quintiq and I sometimes made jokes about what we would name our company if we ever started something together. It's a contraction of MOps and Sops (Marketing Operations and Sales Operations). And thus, SMOps is born. Trend Micro was kind enough to let me invoice a small portion in advance. Payment should be in by the end of January, around the time I would no longer get a salary from Quintiq. With no savings and a mortgage, I'm checking my bank account almost five times per day. I'm that nervous. Luckily, I have a lot of distractions with the exciting work I am doing for Trend Micro.

An agency from the United States implemented Marketo Engage globally. Regions were quickly trained. Though the implementation was done quite professionally in my opinion, it's not successful in some of the regions. Simply providing a new tool, even combined with training, does not result in magical success and/or change. Armed with a platform like Marketo, European marketers are looking at me to help them succeed in Europe. The quality of leads for sales needs to improve. And they need more new names. But all of that should be accomplished without any extra headcount. Barry and I start working to improve the lead management process in order to improve the quality of the leads. I productize their best-practice campaigns into example campaigns. Examples they could easily clone. This will allow them to do more campaigns without the need for additional resources.

"Marketers say that the biggest benefit of automation is saving time."

Venture Harbour

"Marketing automation drives a 14.5% increase in sales productivity and a 12.2% reduction in marketing overhead."

SalesFusion, Invespcro

I suggest running partner webinars to get more new names in. Thus far, they conducted four webinars a year earlier. We set out to conduct about four or five webinar topics. For each topic, we will do the webinar multiple times, each time with a different regional channel partner of Trend Micro. This allows both Trend Micro and the channel partner to exchange leads. Both parties market the webinar on the internet and through their database. Registrants are then available for both parties. Basically, you're exchanging a portion of your interested databases.

"Webinars with partners allow you to tap into interested leads from your partner's database."

A total of forty-five webinars are conducted in the first year. About twice as many campaigns were conducted compared to a year earlier, resulting in more than double the number of new names. Together with the improved lead management process, about five times more sales-ready leads are generated.

What Does It Take to Run Webinars?

I get this question many times. Watch the videos below to learn about:

- Getting started with webinars
- Five steps to optimize your webinar strategy
- How to generate leads with online events
- Engaging webinar formats
- Benefits of integrating your webinar platform with marketing automation

Trend Micro
Customer Story

Video: How to deliver an
engaging webinar that
works

Video: Behind the
scenes of a webinar

After my work for Trend Micro, I still have a few days available. I'm able to welcome several new customers throughout 2016. I help Planon with email preferences, and I help an old Quintiq colleague at Graydon with templates. I also get a call from a marketer at PinkRoccade. I met her at a roundtable a year earlier. She mentions they recently had Marketo Engage technically implemented and now want to make the next steps. Instead of figuring everything out themselves, they would like to leverage best practices straight away.

Together with another marketer at PinkRoccade, we manage to book some successes. More business units at PinkRoccade would like to participate. Even other brands from Total Specific Solutions (TSS) would like to participate. Working with different entities and brands, sometimes even competing ones, brings more complex challenges than simply working with regions and/or business units. How could I leverage "Workspaces & Partitions" for this in Marketo Engage? It's an enterprise feature, while the different entities at TSS are more like medium-sized businesses.

Each brand does not have the skills and manpower to manage its own templates. So I centralized all the templates in a global workspace and shared each template with the matching brand workspace. This allows each brand to have its own environment, brand, database, and campaigns, but everything is still managed from a global perspective, without the need for high-end local skills.

I notice the demand for my services is growing. Still, freelancing comes with limitations. Some companies do not outsource critical work to an *einzelganger*. But even more challenging is coping with customers that want to start their project before your previous project is finished. Moving from one project to another often results in working days longer than twelve hours. Alternatively, sometimes you don't have any work for weeks in between projects. I have two ideas to deal with this.

PinkRoccade
Customer Story

The first idea is for companies to outsource their Marketo Engage campaign deployment to me. It's not high-end consulting work. It's also not fully in line with my ideas to help others succeed. The hourly rate I can ask for is also lower. But it does provide a steadier stream of income. Trend Micro is one of the first customers for campaign deployment.

I now have a project three days per week. And I have about two days per week for campaigning work. Perfect! Not really though. I quickly realize that the two days of campaigning work are spread over the five days of the week. Again, I find myself working ten-to-twelve-hour days. I then reach out to a freelancer who I know from the user group. She spent three years executing Marketo Engage campaigns at Xebia. She would like to travel the world and work remotely. My campaign work could be ideal for her. Though I do struggle with how a new face and the time zone delays will affect my customers.

Campaigns created in Marketo Engage by her or myself are still of better quality than what I see in the market though. I see a lot of marketing automation platform customers that outsource campaign concepts to advertising agencies. These agencies excel in coming up with brilliant campaigns and content. But then they try to deploy their content in many different automation platforms with only superficial know-how. This causes so many mistakes in logic and data.

"If you operate a marketing automation platform, please make sure you can deploy campaigns yourself."

If you operate a marketing automation platform, please make sure you can deploy campaigns yourself. Invest in knowledge and expertise. Or outsource the campaign deployment to an agency that excels in the platform you operate in. For example, Leaseweb outsources Marketo Engage campaign work to SMOps in the spring of 2016. I subcontract a former Quintiq colleague for this. Another example is where I help a Marketo agency from the United States with campaign work for one of their international customers in Amsterdam.

I now have many years of relevant experience in the software industry. I know that software can scale quickly. So my second idea is to productize some of the add-ons I developed for Marketo Engage. The first one is CalcItNow. I keep stretching the limits. As a result, I sometimes run into limitations on certain platforms. One of the limitations in Marketo Engage is that you can only add or subtract scores. I wanted to also multiply and divide. Why? For every month of inactivity, I want to reduce the lead score by 10% rather than a fixed number. Otherwise, a lead with a very high score from the past, despite not being active for over a year, could have a higher score than a recent lead.

CalcItNow is a math lab not only for Marketo Engage but also for other platforms. I manage to get several clients in, and I now find myself split between consulting and software, where consulting gives me more energy than the software business.

A few months before I left Quintiq, Quintiq was acquired by Dassault Systèmes. While Quintiq has their state-of-the-art marketing automation work based on Marketo Engage and Salesforce, Dassault Systèmes is still running Neolane and Siebel on premises. Dassault Systèmes wants to set up a best-practice marketing automation environment for all its other subsidiaries. What can they learn from the successes of Quintiq? They approached and contracted me for this. A team of leaders and experts from Quintiq and Dassault Systèmes is formed to prepare a variety of workshops in Den Bosch and Paris. The marketing automation best-practices workshops are joined by leadership and experts from different teams (e.g., Demand Generation, Field Marketing, Marketing Operations, Sales Operations, etc.).

Dassault Systèmes
Customer Story

Business as a freelancer is going well, and I have a lot of work. When Silvy and I met in 2005, we couldn't afford a dream wedding. So we only got legally married before Suze was born in 2010. Now Iza is five years old, and Suze is seven years old. Any significant event, such as a wedding, would be something they could potentially still remember when they are older. So on June 9, 2017, Silvy and I have our dream wedding together with our daughters.

A third option emerges in mid-2017. A former colleague from TiasNimbas reaches out to me. She is a lecturer for International Business Studies at Fontys University of Applied Sciences. She asks me to cocreate and teach a new "Digital Sales & Marketing Innovation" elective. Together with a few others, I set up the content for the next class. Next to teaching myself, I also invite multiple guest speakers, such as Rob from Quintiq and someone from Marketo. Helping the next generation gives me a lot of energy. And that's a good thing, as it isn't very attractive from a financial perspective.

Near the end of the first semester, I want to give one of the students the opportunity to do an internship at SMOps. Again, another way for me to help someone. That student will then be able to gain relevant real-life knowledge about marketing operations. SMOps is still just me in my attic at home. No place to welcome an intern. However, I recently joined the OZO, a local entrepreneur's society. I did this to meet other entrepreneurs and exchange ideas on entrepreneurship. Who else can you talk to to figure out what it takes to hire your first intern and/or employee? One of the board members convinced me it was the ideal group for me.

I meet two members at an OZO meeting. Both have an office in the same building. I call the owner, and he still has one room left, which I can rent. Next to the OZO, it's another way for me to surround myself with other entrepreneurs and create an environment where I can potentially learn and grow. I meet Dave, and he shows me the room. The building is situated on what used to be real estate from Galvanitas, a company managed and coowned by my grandfather. It's the perfect spot to take the next steps with SMOps. And a perfect spot for my first intern, who starts after the summer of 2017.

I still think about continuity. I have some software customers, but I don't get any energy from my software business. I also have contracts for campaign deployment, and I lecture at Fontys. But what if I fall ill for one year? I do have proper insurance for this. But when I'm able to get back to work, I wouldn't have any customers and/or pipeline left. I need to grow my business with employees to secure more continuity. Not just for myself but also for my customers. But I do realize it's replacing one sort of stress with another. I start to investigate the source of my revenues and successes to prepare for growth.

Where Trend Micro was a game-changer as a launching customer, Essent is the customer that makes the next phase possible in the summer of 2017. I receive a weekly Google Search update on new search results with the keyword *Marketo*. Essent is looking for a Marketo developer, so I go to meet up with the team at Essent. They have already selected Marketo Engage. They are looking for an expert to join the team to roll out the platform. In me, they see a possibility to not only technically roll out Marketo Engage but also leverage best practices.

Essent, pressured by energy market forces, chose a direction that asked for specific marketing capabilities. Along the complete value chain of the energy market, different forces put pressure on the profitability of Essent B2B, which resulted in a loss-making business segment for Essent. For the first time in the market, Essent is now serving large B2B customers online in a newly developed application and customer information system called Unity. Because of that, Essent needed to support the execution of campaigns for acquisition and retention.

The different energy market forces in play:

- Decrease in consumption due to decentral production
- High cost to serve due to customer-specific exceptions
- Intermediary detracts value in the value chain
- Customers focus on sustainability & energy efficiency

The minimum viable product (MVP) and many stretch objectives for Marketo are achieved in just three sprints, integrating multiple customer information systems, analytics, SMS, third-party apps, and channels. I couldn't have done it without the great team at Essent.

"Try to start executing a campaign during implementation. Not only to let stakeholders experience automation right away but also to cookie your existing database. This enables you to start tracking behavior for your already existing database."

Throughout the three sprints, we have already executed multiple very successful campaigns. One of the campaigns was related to direct debit. There was a need to (re)confirm direct debit for migrated customers, limiting the number of calls by the operations team.

In total, 2,536 customers were contacted by email (44% on DD, 56% without DD), and 1,239 responded (49%) to confirm the direct debit status for the new contract. Many hours were saved by not manually contacting hundreds of customers to reconfirm direct debit. And the number of total customers with direct debit increased significantly.

Essent -
Implementation
Case Study

Halfway through the Marketo project at Essent, I find myself on a boat on the canals of Utrecht. I'm there with about ten other Dutch Marketo User Group members. I receive a call from the freelancer I contracted earlier on. She was contacted by Youwe, a digital agency in the Netherlands. They are looking for someone with marketing automation expertise and Salesforce experience to subcontract on a project for a customer of theirs.

The customer, Staples EMEA, wants to prepare a marketing automation business case for their complex international matrix organization as part of their digital change. The lead consultant from Youwe and I work together with the team from Staples EMEA. Through in-depth interviews and workshops designed to expose the high-value use cases, the IT landscape is mapped, and a marketing automation road map is defined.

"Sixty-three percent of businesses that outgrow their competitors use marketing automation."

The Lenskold Group

I continue to collect more and more marketing automation best practices. And I know why implementing a marketing automation platform, even when combined with training, will not result in success. But are there more examples of how not to approach marketing automation?

Staples
Customer Story

This Chapter's Challenges	This Chapter's Solutions
How to help others succeed?	Think about consulting, freelancing, lecturing, and/or hiring interns.
How to start freelancing?	Find a launching customer.
Why does implementing a platform, even when combined with training, not result in success/change?	Implementation is the first and smallest step. You then need to leverage it.
How to easily generate new names with a small budget?	Webinars with partners allow you to tap into interested leads from your partner's database.
How to get more balanced income streams as a freelancer?	Think about products and services people could structurally outsource to you.
How to take the first step in hiring extra resources?	First, think about subcontracting other freelancers or hiring interns.
Why do some businesses grow, while others do not?	For me, it was about genuinely helping others succeed and getting energy from that.
How to mitigate risks as a freelancer and/or a small, growing business?	Reserve enough time to reflect and think about the future. Which risks can you mitigate?
Why do some projects advance your company, while others don't?	Stretch the limits in projects. Think beyond the scope and simple execution. Truly think about success. These successes will create reference cases that can propel your business.

WHEN MARKETING AUTOMATION DOESN'T WORK

It's early 2018 when Arjen Segers starts frequently visiting my office in Oosterhout. I met Arjen at a Marketo User Group meeting in Utrecht the year before. He works as the digital marketing manager for Korn Ferry in Brussels, and he frequently travels to their Amsterdam office. My office is about halfway through his trip and right next to the freeway. Arjen heard about my trips to the Marketing Nation Summit in San Francisco every year, and he wants to go to expand his knowledge. He also wants to get Marketo Engage certified on-site. In all those years that I went to the United States, I'd never seen more than San Francisco's Financial District and Fisherman's Wharf. So I propose that we go on a road trip together in the days before the Marketing Nation Summit. It will provide us with a way to see more of the United States, and it provides Arjen an opportunity to study for his exam and ask me questions about it while I drive.

To keep nonbusiness expenses to a minimum, we book a flight to Las Vegas with a nineteen-hour stopover in Los Angeles. We spend the afternoon at Manhattan Beach before heading back to the airport to catch our flight to Las Vegas. The next day, we pick up our rental car at Las Vegas Airport. We drive through Death Valley, Sequoia Park, and Yosemite Park, and eventually, we end up on the west coast. We take the scenic route through 17-Mile Drive and stop at Pebble Beach along the way. We have plenty of time to talk about our marketing automation experiences, and Arjen has plenty of time to study for his Marketo Engage certification exam. We arrive in San Francisco on Saturday morning, the day before the summit starts. We meet up with my coleader of the Dutch Marketo User Group, Maarten Westdorp. Maarten and I have known each other for years and have visited quite a few summits together. We hop on an old Gillibus with about twenty other Marketo Champions© for a wine tasting tour in Napa Valley and Sonoma before the summit starts on Sunday.

On the last day of the summit, just a few hours before my flight back, I meet up with a German account executive from Marketo. He's responsible for sales in the German-speaking region of Europe. We've known each other for quite a while now. He and the VP of Sales for Continental Europe would like me to assist in the sales process of a potential new customer in Germany. It's a big multinational that wants to improve its digital marketing and sales. They want to start a pilot in the Netherlands first. Both think that a Dutch-speaking marketing automation and Marketo Engage expert can potentially make a difference in the sales process.

Since leaving Quintiq, I now have done a variety of marketing automation projects and implementations. And I have exchanged experiences with so many marketing automation professionals around the world. I'm starting to untangle when marketing automation is successful and when it fails.

I see that companies think that owning a marketing automation platform magically drives more revenue. People think technology solves their challenges without any additional effort. But without any professional guidance, it typically takes at least a few months before you can start to see the first measurable results. Too often, I see impatient leaders pressure marketing teams when they don't see any results after the first three months after purchasing their marketing automation platform. So be fair and manage expectations. You're in this for the long run! It takes time for your digital maturity to grow.

"Seventy-nine percent of top-performing companies have been using marketing automation for three or more years."

Venture Harbour

Also, think about the psychology behind adapting marketing automation into the lives, thoughts, and practical day-to-day of marketers. Why does it often seem so hard? How can organizations utilize all that potential?

The summit is over, and I'm back in the Netherlands. Not long after, Essent reaches out to me. The small-medium-enterprise segment of Essent is inspired by the work done with Marketo Engage at the large-enterprise segment of Essent. A new project team is formed.

On the job at Essent, I receive a phone call from Jacques van Seeters. He's contracted by HVC, a waste management company owned by over forty municipalities, to set up and manage their new energy company. Jacques and Leon Harrewijn selected Marketo Engage as their marketing automation platform. They realize that innovation in digital is a must-have for the energy company to become successful. I want to come over to their office, but Jacques insists on coming to my office in Oosterhout.

Looking out of the window in my office, he points his finger to a small bungalow on the former Galvanitas property. "I lived there as a child, as my father was the sales manager at Galvanitas." I can't believe what I'm hearing. Jacques was not only born and raised in Oosterhout but also has a connection with Galvanitas. I tell him my grandfather used to be coowner and managing director. He remembers playing with some of my uncles as kids. We instantly connect.

Jacques is in his fifties. He has a lot of business experience. He once set up and managed EnergieDirect, a subsidiary of Essent. And he founded a solar company before starting his interim position at HVC. His expertise is in making innovations in marketing and sales.

"The company that best manages automation will be the likely winner in its industry."

He recognizes that marketing automation is a game-changer. The company that best manages automation will be the likely winner in its industry. Craftmanship is one of his core values. So Jacques contracts biweekly marketing automation coaching hours with the Marketo Engage implementation project. Jacques often stays at my office after the coaching sessions. We talk a lot about my growth ideas and the development of the services.

I'm now getting more requests than I can handle on my own. And the type of work is not something I can subcontract to another freelancer. I decide to hire my first employee. I make a list of people in my network that are proficient in Marketo Engage. There are two candidates I consider for the job. It's important to me to choose the right first employee because they will impact future culture. I'm happy to hear that Fianna van Dijk is equally enthusiastic as I am. But I will have to wait till August 2018 before she can start.

Just before the summer, the German account executive at Marketo reaches out to me again. They refer to the conversation we had at the Marketing Nation Summit earlier that year. They reveal the prospect. It's DHL Express. DHL Express has narrowed down the shortlist to only two platforms. For each platform, there will be a two-day proof of concept (POC). There's a whole team behind the scenes at Marketo that prepares the POC environment. On-site, I meet up with two senior consultants from Marketo. Together we talk through the final preparations.

At DHL Express, I enter a room with about twenty people. They just completed the other platform's POC over the two days before. The other platform is their benchmark now. In the first few hours, I remain relatively quiet. I don't want to disrupt the Marketo consultants, as this seems like an important sales process to Marketo. But we realize our approach thus far is not working as we expected. We overhaul everything over lunch. I notice quite a few people are simply evaluating the platform based on the user interface. Good ease of use is helpful of course, and it might result in a shorter adoption period. But in my opinion, it's just a fraction of what's important when selecting your marketing automation platform.

"How is the marketing automation platform going to enable your transformation?"

There are more important topics. How is the marketing automation platform going to enable your transformation? How is it going to grow with you? Which use cases can be realized? I start to share anecdotes of previous successes and failures. And we discuss the many tips on how marketing automation could work for DHL Express.

"Eighty-six percent pay attention to the 'ease of use' as to the most important factor while choosing a long-term marketing automation solution."

Regalix

Day two is over. It's out of our hands now. The four of them decide to go out to dinner at a great Japanese restaurant in Amsterdam. We concluded we turned things around on day two—a turnaround that eventually results in a call from DHL Express at the end of the summer.

The Global Head of Digital Marketing & Communications at DHL Express calls me. She mentions they selected Marketo Engage as their marketing automation platform. They intend to pilot the platform in the Netherlands. It's a big project, especially due to their wish to connect their bespoke CRM. She hired Marketo Professional Services for work on data and integration. But she wants to contract SMOps for migrating and onboarding the Netherlands to the new platform. And she also kind of wants me to be a second pair of eyes on the DHL side to evaluate and add to work done by Marketo. I call Arjen to fully join SMOps. We kick-off a great four-month project and work with and meet great people like Katja Keesom, Pieter van Ouwerkerk, and many more.

Within just thirty days, I go from freelancer with ad-hoc subcontractors, to a three FTE company. After Trend Micro and Essent, DHL Express is the third big catalyst in the growth of my agency.

With the acceleration in growth, my discussions with Jacques reach the next level. I believe he can play a crucial role in our growth. Jacques wants to take on a commercial role so I can focus on quality and delivery. Jacques, with craftmanship as one of his core values, wants to use his first year on projects to gain as much experience as possible. Jacques starts part-time in October 2018, gradually building up to full-time by January 1, 2019.

DHL Express
Customer Story

Meanwhile, with Jacques leaving, HVC wants to expand the use of Marketo Engage to production communications. They want to communicate with customers about submitting their annual electricity usage, annual contract renewal, annual invoices, and such. This comes with some requirements. HVC needs to have access to contract, usage, and connection data in Marketo Engage. Luckily, Marketo Engage is one of the enterprise-worthy marketing automation platforms that sufficiently supports custom objects.

> "Thirty-four percent of marketing professionals think data integration is the biggest barrier to marketing automation."

Adestra

With every new project, I see more and more patterns for success. It's not just about a great marketing automation implementation, even if best practices are used. It's about how you're able to leverage the platform afterward. Change management plays a crucial role in marketing automation success (e.g., How do you activate your staff?).

"Change management plays a crucial role in marketing automation success."

I look at my notes and sketches from the past several years. I finally see the pattern. I can finally visualize it. I create a new visual, which I store in my growth strategy deck for SMOps. The low-res sketch below is a predecessor of what will later become Chaploop™.

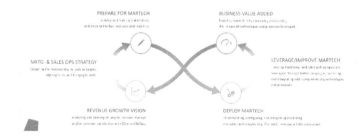

As mentioned earlier, digital transformation comes down to four key areas. Change management is one of those areas. Data is another area that I see so many failures in. Marketing automation is only as good as the data it uses. Still, I rarely see marketing teams budgeting for data quality. We did have some small projects to fix poor data (e.g., at Planon). Eventually, one of the first bigger data quality projects was implemented at Essent. They have many duplicates from their list uploads, but cleaning those is tricky because some of them are intended duplicates.

"The costs of bad data in the U.S. alone is more than $3 trillion per year."

Harvard Business Review

"Marketing and sales professionals believe more than 30% of their records are incorrect in some way. This problem manifests itself often as a barrier to marketing across multiple channels. 42% say inaccurate contact data is the biggest barrier to multichannel marketing."

eConsultancy.com: The Cost Of Bad Data Stats

Essent - Data
Case Study

How Bad Data Enters Your Marketing Automation

I see two typical sources of bad data in marketing automation platforms. The first source is sales manually entering values into an integrated CRM platform. Some examples are:

- Guestimating a person's email address at the company
- Putting in an *X*, when not knowing a person's first name
- Unintentional typos
- Allowing multiple languages to be used in the same field

The second source comes from leads entering data through forms. This type of data can vary from unintentional typos to mixed languages in fields.

"Use picklists instead of open text fields whenever you can!"

It's best to prevent bad data from entering in the first place. So use picklists in CRM and forms instead of open text fields whenever possible. You can also clean and normalize bad data after the fact. Simply utilize workflows in your marketing automation platform (e.g., turn "the Netherlands", "Holland", or "Nederland" into "Netherlands" to normalize the field "Country").

"The global average decay rate is 3% per month. So that is one third of your database every year. In some industries this can be as high as 6%."

aiThority.com

How Data Turns Bad over Time

So you've managed to prevent bad data from entering. And you have processes running to fix bad data after the fact. But you're not there yet. Your data decays over time. Data that is good today can turn bad a few months from now.

Some examples are:

- Unsubscribes
- Bounces
- People changing jobs
- Companies that go out of business
- Loss of relevance
- Updates to picklist values, while not updating old data

Poor data will result in poor marketing performance. So it's important to constantly monitor the health of your data.

"Constantly monitor the health of your data."

Select your ten to fifteen most used fields for audience selection and/or personalization. What percentage of your database has a value for these fields? And what percentage of your database has a value according to the official picklist values for the corresponding field? Keep monitoring those percentages and act when they drop below an acceptable level.

Poor data is just one of the reasons marketing automation fails. I get many calls from marketing automation customers that are looking for a second opinion. They are not experiencing any value from their platform. They're thinking about switching to a cheaper alternative. The cheaper alternative is not magically going to make a difference. The platform is not the problem. The way the platform was rolled out at their company is most often the cause. They fell into what I call the "Toolbox Trap." The marketing automation platform was implemented and trained from a technical perspective—as if the IT department implemented it. But marketing automation is not just a platform. It's also a mindset.

"A fool with a tool is still a fool."

Grady Booch

113

People need guidance in their journey of transformation. Cocreate new processes together. Brainstorm hypotheses for value creation. Test the hypotheses and scale those that work. After a while, they'll see the light, and they will start expanding the way they think. They'll come up with creative new ways of engaging prospects and customers. This requires a certain work ethic, courage, and trust.

Courage, a safe environment to try and fail, and trust also play a big role in taking the first steps in marketing automation. I see marketing leaders struggle with their decision to start utilizing marketing automation or not. They seem to overestimate the complexity of starting. They ask themselves questions like: Do we have enough content? Do we have the right people? Is CRM integration required? Can we maybe do this without involving sales? It is as if they only see the bottlenecks and not the possibilities.

Pieter van Ouwerkerk, marketing director at DHL Express, shared a great quote with me when talking about his epiphanies.

"Starting marketing automation is somewhat like bungee jumping, you simply need to jump and take that leap of faith."

Pieter van Ouwerkerk

There are many ways for marketing automation not to work. And they have to do with poor personalization. It's easy to dynamically use a person's first name to open your emails. But it's not the real essence of personalization that drives high conversions. The content you send should act as the exact answer to a key question your recipient has right then. Or it should at least trigger an awareness of something new.

"Sixty-six percent of customers expect their interactions with brands to be personalized."

Marketo

Unraveling Your Prospects' Buying Journeys

Key questions in your prospects' buying journeys can be unraveled by conducting interviews with your customers. But how do you determine where in the buyer's journey your lead is? This is where the technique of scoring comes in. Scoring isn't just useful for determining a lead's propensity to buy. You can also score other things. Well, if your marketing automation platform supports multiple scoring fields. And if you can build your workflows to impact those additional scoring fields. Then you can score behaviors that match what a lead would do in a specific buying stage (e.g., visit your website's pricing page later in the buyer's journey).

A similar technique can be used to estimate what type of persona a lead is. Is the lead someone with purchasing power? Is the lead your key ambassador at the prospect? Or perhaps a ratifier (e.g., from the legal or procurement department)? Another way is to create workflows to automatically determine "Role" and/or "Department" based on the lead's job title. This will also help you in better targeting your email messages.

Create segmentations for buyer journey stage and persona. The segment with the highest score is most likely representing the truth. Don't forget about other segments like language, region, and industry. They will help you send even better dynamic and personalized messages.

"When an email is not personalized, 52% of customers say they'll find somewhere else to go."

Salesforce

I implement everything into our marketing automation platform, everything involving data quality, data monitoring, personalization, and segmentations. I always implement all our best practices in our marketing automation platform. I believe in "practice what you preach." And we help businesses grow. But what about my own business? How can I further grow my own company?

This Chapter's Challenges	This Chapter's Solutions
Why do some companies not experience any value from implementing marketing automation?	Owning a marketing automation platform does not magically drive more revenue.
How long does it take to generate value from marketing automation?	Don't be impatient for quick results.
What are good or poor marketing automation platform selection criteria?	Don't focus on ease of use. Think about how the platform can enable your transformation.
What is required to understand your audiences?	Data integrations and custom objects enable more relevant conversations.
Where and when should you spend the most effort on marketing automation success?	The real work starts after deployment. That's when you start to leverage the platform. Change management is crucial.
What are your sources of bad data?	Data entry by leads (e.g., in forms) or by sales through CRM. And data quality decays over time.
How to fix bad data entry?	Use picklists in forms and CRM where possible.
How to address data decay?	Stay on top of your data health by monitoring your most crucial fields.

What prevents companies from starting with marketing automation?	Marketing automation complexity is often overestimated. Take small steps toward success. Test hypotheses and scale those that work. Don't try to build a 100% solution from the start.
What causes poor marketing automation performance?	A "Dear {{lead.First Name}}" personalized email is not always a recipe for success. Find out a lead's genuine interests. Use scoring techniques combined with segmentations to detect persona and buying journey stage.

GROWING THE BUSINESS

The year is nearly over when we get the opportunity to move into the entire upper floor of the office building. We urgently need a meeting room and more than just three desks. I work throughout the Christmas holiday to prepare the floor.

We're starting to get more recognition. Customers share their experiences working with us and why they are satisfied. However, there's a total disconnect between those accounts and how we present ourselves on our website, a website that I built hastily in the weeks before I started freelancing with my first customer, Trend Micro. That obviously needs to change. We're also taken more seriously in the marketing automation space, while our company name, SMOps, is just a gimmick. It's time for a big change.

The following section has little to do with marketing automation. But I do like to share the process that we went through. It might be useful to you when you're thinking about starting your own company, starting your own agency, or rebranding.

"Need a new company name? First, start with unravelling who you truly are."

Don't start with a new name! Start with unraveling who you are! Jacques proposes that we use a variant of the brand pyramid for this.

Rebranding

<u>Core Values</u>

Core values are a vital tool that will help you define the very essence of your brand. There are many variations to explore on the internet. A blog post by INSEAD comes closest to what we use:

1. What type of work and projects do we see now and in the future?
2. What are the functional benefits for us and our customers?
3. What are the emotional benefits? How do they make people feel?
4. Group the core values. Do they differentiate us from competitors?
5. Can we further condense the core values into a purpose?

All four of us keep clustering sticky notes until, in the second session, we define three main clusters for core values: clear, stretching the limits, and for your personal success. Combined, these form our purpose: for your personal success with MarTech.

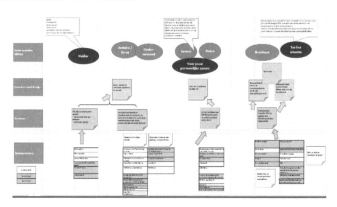

INSEAD
Brand Pyramid

A New Company Name

One week later, after fully digesting the unraveling of our core values and purpose, we have our third session. It's time to choose a new name—a name that matches our identity. Jacques and I have already done a lot of preparation. Jacques suggested using somebody's name in our new company name. This is to reflect "personal." It should be something around technology, innovation, and performance. We turn to Formula 1, probably the most cutting-edge sport in the world. From the whole list of names, there's one name that both of us prefer. It's Colin Chapman. The legendary F1 designer at Lotus who won seven world championships as a constructor.

> "A racing car has only one objective: to win motor races. If it does not do this, it is nothing but a waste of time, money, and effort. That says it all."
>
> *Colin Chapman*

We both agree our new company name should at least contain "Colin" or "Chapman." But we have more criteria, especially with the lessons we learned from our current name, "SMOps":

- It should be relatively easy to pronounce after reading.
- It should have an international feeling.
- It should sound reliable.
- It should fit our three core values.
- It should be a name that will easily stick.
- It should be a likable name that has emotion.

The four of us write close to a hundred sticky notes, which we cluster on the glass wall in our office. There is one name that stands out to all four of us. That is "Chapman & Bright." Bright sounds like a name, but it's derived from one of our core values, "Clear." But it feels a bit elitist and perhaps a bit too old. We drop the ampersand, and the four of us each have a smile on our faces. "Chapman Bright" is here!

Colors and Logo

It's now time to visualize the brand. Jacques prepares by listing and analyzing all our competitors. What colors do they use? Meanwhile, I'm looking into what colors would be appropriate. Blue is the obvious color for IT and for consulting. It reflects trust and reliability. No wonder that over 40% of our competitors also use blue. We have a lot of passion and energy and want to stretch the limits. Orange reflects energy. And it's hardly used by the competition. Though I'm quite comfortable with the Adobe suite and with Microsoft Office, we realize we do need some professional help with visualizing our new brand. We turn to local brand strategist Flaim. Typically, they help with all the things we just completed ourselves. We could have saved ourselves some time with their help, but we also enjoyed the exercise.

Flaim creates three mood boards, from which we picked and refined our new logo. We opt for a font that is rounded and more friendly. We want to stay away from the sharp fonts used by law firms and accountants. The basis of our brand is dark blue, a color we also use for anything related to strategy. Our tag line is orange. Orange, an energetic color, is used to underline things. To make a point. We realize we need a tagline that says something about who we are and what we do, as nobody knows Chapman Bright yet. We settle on "MarTech Fanatics," which also links back to stretching the limits. We choose a shade of green that is often used in healthcare as our supporting color. Healthcare is a people business and fits well with our value of personal success. It's also the color we'll use for anything in operations.

Visuals and Templates

We need visuals to support our identity. Formula 1 works for now, but we shouldn't build the entire story around race cars. We zoom out and realize that we can use anything in endurance sports (e.g., speed skating, relay racing, cycling, etc.), especially endurance sports where there's a team effort. Where a team of specialists helps the athlete win. With a few iterations, Paul's team creates templates for letters and presentations. And they create a briefing for a new website.

A New Website

We unraveled our core values and our purpose. We have a new company name. We have a new logo. We have brand guidelines, colors, and visuals. We also have templates for invoices, letters, and presentations. But all of that can only be experienced by our current customers. We need the materials for our future customers. We need a new website and fast. The Adobe Summit in London is just two months from now. That's our chance for an instant launch of our new brand. We only have one chance to make a great first impression. So I turn to another local I know pretty well. Nick van Gils owns and manages a small digital agency. We have multiple sessions for UI and UX. We want something special. Not something that looks like an edited open-source template. We want something that reflects that it was custom built for us. Something with high quality. And something that fits our identity. Like our fonts, we want the website to have rounded elements to make it softer, more human. We spend most of our rebranding budget on our new website. And I spend most of my time on the website. I write over one hundred pages of content in a matter of weeks. And I also make sure everything on the old website redirects to the new website.

Launching Chapman Bright

Adobe acquired Marketo a year earlier. To prepare for my first Adobe EMEA Summit, I visited my first Adobe Summit in Las Vegas in early 2019. Many of my fellow Marketo Engage Champions© started agencies over the years, especially in the United States. I catch up with my fellow Marketo Champions© and the owners of one of the most well-known Marketo-only agencies in the United States. They are hosting a special Marketo Engage content day in parallel to the Adobe Summit. It's my inspiration for organizing something in London. Still in Las Vegas, I call the owner of the best Marketo Engage agency in Germany. We meet up at the conference hotel terrace. We agree to host an event together in London. Where the Las Vegas conference still has over seventy Marketo Engage sessions, the conference in London will only have eight Marketo Engage sessions. And I'll already present one of those myself.

Video Marketing

We update our customers on our new company name, and we have already started using our new branded materials. But we'll be launching our new brand for the outside world at the London Summit. We want the experience and our investment to last longer than just the summit itself. And we want a bigger audience than just the attendees of our side event. I propose that we shoot a movie after. A short movie that summarizes lessons and information from our side event and the summit itself. But it must be equally as professional as our other branded materials.

"Viewers retain 95% of a message when they watch it in a video, compared to 10% when reading it in text."

Insivia

Jacques's son is nearly finished with his degree in media. His expertise is arranging music, so we ask him to write a tune for our logo bumper and the background music for our videos. He proposes something funky, as he thinks that best reflects our identity. One of his fellow students created the logo animation for our bumper. He incorporates the rising *G* into the animation. The rising *G* imitates a rising sun, which relates to a bright new day. He also joins us in London as the videographer. Arjen helps him out with a whole list of topics and interviews to film.

Watch
the aftermovie

I'm enthusiastic about video marketing. Writing does allow you to share more in-depth content, but video is a great platform for me to share knowledge, as a lot of professionals use video to learn new skills.

"Sixty-five percent of people use online video to help them solve a problem. Want to build a house or remove weird parasites from your eye? YouTube might have the answer."

Google

"Fifty-nine percent of executives say they would rather watch a video than read text."

Wordstream

Companies seem to consider video materials expensive and thus something only bigger companies can do. But we've done multiple videos as a small company. There must be a way to make others aware of the possibilities of video marketing. I get in touch with our video marketing platform TwentyThree, and they ask me to present what I've learned about starting and growing with video marketing at their video marketing meetup (VMM) in Amsterdam.

VMM
slidedeck

Integrate Your Marketing Automation with Your Video Marketing Platform

We now have quite a few videos. But in our marketing automation platform, I can only see who clicked email hyperlinks to those videos or who clicked on a hyperlink to a video on our website. But do they also watch the video? And do they watch the entire video or just a portion? What does that say about their interest, intent, and/or propensity to buy? How can I improve our lead-scoring algorithms? Choose a video marketing platform that can easily integrate with your marketing automation platform. It allows you to do the following:

- Integrate forms in videos to capture new names
  - Before being able to start the video
  - After a certain timeframe to continue watching
  - Optionally at the end of the video
- Leverage your tracking cookie to identify who's watching what
- Trigger workflows when someone watches a video
- Adjust scoring for people who watch a minimum percentage
- Add calls to action in videos in sync with your automation

"Eighty-one percent of businesses use video as marketing tool."

HubSpot

A video marketing platform still allows you to share your videos on YouTube or LinkedIn. And it also ingests statistics from platforms like YouTube, for example. It still provides you with vital insights into how your videos perform.

I'm happy with the launch of Chapman Bright and how video played a role in the launch. But I realize a lot of the company's growth is still connected to my thought leadership. For Chapman Bright to grow, it needs to have its own recognition. I need to take a step back for that to happen. It allows my colleagues and Chapman Bright to step into the spotlight. I plan to not do any videos and/or keynotes in the upcoming months.

I want to further grow the business to land more intellectually challenging projects and to provide more continuity for myself and our customers. But how much do I want Chapman Bright to grow? And how? Jacques and I agree that a company between ten and twenty-five people in size is the sweet spot. That's big enough to be robust but small enough to have a personal atmosphere.

Many years ago, I focused on existing Marketo Engage customers to get more out of their platform. I differentiated based on my recognized expertise. Working for these customers resulted in repeatable best practices, best practices we then used to target companies that were considering Marketo Engage and wanted a best-practice implementation. In turn, the work on these customers resulted in highly satisfied customer projects. Projects that go far beyond the Marketo Engage platform. We help to improve and digitally transform marketing and sales for customers by constantly testing hypotheses from a MarTech viewpoint and scaling those that create value. It's time to also focus on the awareness phase of marketing automation.

Deloitte once mentioned they wouldn't contract an *einzelganger*, but I'm not alone anymore. They reach out to us with a very specific challenge. Every country has its own MarTech stack. They are centralizing to a single Salesforce instance for their CRM. Several countries use Marketo Engage, and most of these use a native integration with their local Salesforce. The native integration is pretty good and requires little investment to set up. But there are downsides. You can only connect one instance. And once you connect, Marketo Engage inherits the data architecture of Salesforce. This in turn shuts down several endpoints in Marketo Engage, including the "Company" endpoint. This also makes it impossible to move to a custom integration (e.g., through middleware).

There's only one solution. Deloitte must spin up a new instance, which they can connect with Salesforce through middleware, such as Mulesoft. Deloitte wants support with the required Salesforce integration, as well as with how to spin up the new instance. Their instance is several years old and contains a lot of legacy and waste. It's the perfect time for a fresh and clean start.

I see many MarTech customers, especially marketing automation customers, that run their platform for longer than five or even ten years. At the same time, things are poorly documented, and different administrators inherit the platform from their predecessors. An annual housekeeping exercise can keep your instance fresh. But it will only last a few years. At some point, you're dealing with too much legacy material and too many outdated concepts and processes; it's time to spin up a new instance and only migrate your best practices.

> *"At some point, you're dealing with too much legacy material and too many outdated concepts and processes in your marketing automation platform; it's time to spin up a new instance and only migrate your best practices."*

Not too long after Deloitte, we get in touch with Magnitude, an international software company. They have acquired multiple brands over the last years. Their potential is locked in the possibility of cross-selling the different products between the customers of these brands. But each brand still uses its own marketing tools. It's time to consolidate to a company standard. This will allow Magnitude to easily engage all customers across the different brands. They are already consolidating to Salesforce for their CRM. And they have already chosen to use Marketo Engage as their main marketing automation platform.

Deloitte
Customer Story

We propose two options for them to choose from. Spin up a new and fresh Marketo Engage instance or continue with the Marketo Engage instance they already have for a few brands. There are limitations in the available time, budget, and in-house expertise at that time. So they choose to continue with the current instance.

There's big news during the final user acceptance tests (UAT) of the consolidation project. The former leadership of the acquired brands leaves the company, and the new owner truly recognizes the importance of a centralized MarTech stack, including in-house expertise. He is an expert from the United States, and he manages to convince the leadership of the importance of investing in a fresh, new Marketo Engage instance. He's more than qualified to manage this on his own from the United States without our help.

Before starting the project at Magnitude, I receive a call from Katja Keesom. We work together at DHL Express, and she also attended the London Summit. She even provided quotes for our movie. She tells me she kept thinking about the ideas I shared during the summit on how to further grow Chapman Bright. She's been at DHL Express for nearly twenty years now. But she's so enthusiastic about what we do that we start talking about her joining Chapman Bright.

I think Katja will be a great addition to the team. But she's also a key stakeholder at DHL Express. I'm pretty nervous because I don't want to "steal" my customer's staff. Especially not if the person in question is also one of our ambassadors and key stakeholders at that customer. This has the potential to completely disrupt the relationship. Katja assures me it's her decision and that everything will work out fine. We both agree she should have the opportunity to properly finish and hand over her work at DHL. But it will take four to five months to do so, so she'll start on November 1, 2019.

Magnitude
Customer Story

While waiting for Katja to join the team, Fianna announces she's pregnant. A Chapman Bright first! Though it is exciting news, it does mean we're now back to three people instead of the projected five. Arjen, Jacques, and I work overtime but achieve minimal margins. Fully contributing to projects, I'm unable to continue to further grow Chapman Bright. I spend about half my time on bookkeeping, invoices, IT, and the like. Jacques and I make a bold move. We start looking for an all-around office manager. After meeting several candidates, we hire Lot, who best fits our core values.

It's still very busy for Arjen, Jacques, and myself. We'll have to wait till the start of November for Katja to start, till mid-November for Fianna to return, and till December 1 for Lot to start. But we do realize that we want to do more to help others succeed and further strengthen our new brand. We want to organize a knowledge day for our customers and other interested people. The "MarTech Fanatics Forum" is planned for the end of November.

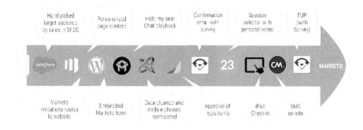

Even though I stepped out of the spotlight to enable colleagues to shine, we do agree I should be the host of the day. And I commit to doing a presentation about leveraging marketing technology to expand engagement beyond the day of your events. My storyline is based around showing how I got the audience in the room and what happened behind the scenes.

Download
my slides

Around the same period, Adobe (previously Marketo) asks the Marketo Champions to contribute to an eBook. The "Marketo Success Series." I contribute to the chapter on how to leverage Marketo Engage for events.

The second half of 2019 must be one of the busiest periods in my career. We're growing to six people, and our office floor will be too small. I ask Dave if I can also rent the floor below us, where our old office room is situated. But things turn around. Dave's business is also growing, and he needs more office space too. He wants to expand into our floor. So we urgently need to find a new office space. As if I wasn't busy enough.

Sometimes luck is just written in the stars. We stumble upon a 120-year-old beer brewery, a national monument. It was vacant, as the owner was finishing up exterior renovations. Jacques isn't convinced that we'll be able to make the interior reflect our quality standards, but I convince him that everything is going to be okay. I find myself, with the help of professional Pascal, spending another Christmas holiday building a new office. But it's going to be amazing!

eBook:
Marketo event
programs

After all these years, after all those ideas and concepts—EventTrips with Edwin during my studies, CalcItNow, Decobox, LastminuteTop100, and many others. Why didn't these ideas flourish? And why does Chapman Bright? I keep thinking about it. All my previous ideas were merely ideas to make money. They were ideas in markets I had no background and/or experience in. Ideas for money without passion. Chapman Bright comes from my passion for helping others succeed. And you know what? It's okay to make money along the way as long as you stay true to your mission. But that's *my* mission. But what about my colleagues at Chapman Bright?

Big Hairy Audacious Goal (BHAG)

I want to ensure we're all on the same path. If we're on the same path, I'm also reaching my goals. I organize two sessions with our team of six to unravel our Big Hairy Audacious Goal (BHAG):

- A BHAG is a compelling, longer-term goal that is intriguing enough to inspire the people of an organization to act.
- A BHAG is meant to energize people to implement a big-picture-type plan that could take a decade to complete. It answers the question: "What gets you out of bed every morning?"
- It originates from the 1994 HarperBusiness book *Built to Last: Successful Habits of Visionary Companies* by Jim Collins and Jerry Porras.

The key thing that comes back throughout our own BHAG sessions is how proud the team is to help guide people to the next level. No matter how small the step. No matter how high or low the maturity level is. We want to be:

"Europe's Leading MarTech Team, Guiding Success Stories."

But how can I operationalize this? How can I embed this in everything we do? How can I productize this in all our work?

This Chapter's Challenges	This Chapter's Solutions
What does it take to grow your business?	Hard work, overtime, and potentially spending Christmas painting office walls.
How to come to genuine core values?	Use the brand pyramid.
How to choose a new company name (or new product name?)	Determine your requirements first, and then build on your core values.
Launching the new brand.	Hard work, overtime, etc.
Can small companies also excel in video marketing?	Video is retained better than text. Many professionals educate themselves through video. It's an ideal medium to share content that helps others succeed.
How can you leverage interactions with your videos by connecting your video platform to your marketing automation?	It allows you to capture new names and to better estimate your audience's intent and interest, which helps you to improve your lead scores.
At some point, you're dealing with too much legacy material and too many outdated concepts and processes in your marketing automation platform.	It's then time to spin up a new instance and only migrate your best practices.
How to expand engagement beyond the day of your event?	Manage your events with marketing automation.
How to energize everybody at the company toward the same goal?	Formulate a big hairy audacious goal (BHAG).

CREATING VALUE PROPOSITIONS

With our additional focus on companies in the awareness phase of starting marketing automation, we have new key buying questions to answer. How to engage C-level executives (CEO and CSO) on the topic of marketing automation? How to convince them it's the right investment (ROI)? These are the questions a digital marketer might have when pitching his or her ideas for marketing automation to leadership. Marketing automation is not the goal; it contributes to achieving a goal. Where should the organization be one, two, and/or five years from now? What does the world look like? How do you see yourself engaging your audiences? What (digital) capabilities do you need to achieve that? And which steps can be taken today toward that goal? And how will those steps today scale in the future? In summary, what does your marketing automation maturity roadmap look like? How to prove the possible contribution to the goal for each item on the roadmap? It's these types of questions, not even addressing actual marketing automation requirements, that play a critical role in my next steps.

> *"Marketing automation is not the goal; marketing automation contributes to achieving your goals."*

In parallel to further tuning my methodology, Chaploop™, I want to package each of our value-adding services into growth plans. I want to define phases to grow toward. And I want to leverage my methodology for continuous growth to reach those maturity levels. Each item on the roadmap must fit into one or more of the four pillars for digital transformation success (technology, process, data, and change management). Each service must be a genuine recipe for success. We already have so much, so I wouldn't call it product development. I'd rather call it product refinement. But we also need to find customers to make successful with these refined services. I set out to create a value proposition document for each of our services.

What Should Be Included in a Value Proposition Document?

- The core of the value-added service in just two to three sentences
- Key questions for each buyer persona for each buying stage
- Research, statistics, and quotes
- Prerequisites for a customer
- What's the added value of answering the key questions?
- Categorized proposition ingredients (our services)
- Required resources and investment for the customer
- Business case (the added value versus investment)
- Possible objections and reasons not to buy
- Maturity roadmap
- Sales tactics (according to market type—e.g., new solution)
- Marketing tactics (according to market type)
- Content to be created based on all chapters of this document

I also want to validate everything with customers and fellow experts. It takes a lot of time to finish a single value proposition document. But that's when the work starts. We need to create a webpage for every proposition. And we write out all the elements of the proposition in a factsheet, which can be downloaded by a prospect. For every proposition, I easily come up with over twenty pieces of content to create. We have hundreds of pieces of content to create. This is going to take years. Prioritization based on impact versus effort will be vital.

With the first pieces of content created, I can start to think about marketing automation. I get crazy enthusiastic. I'm back where I started all those years ago—investigating key questions from buyer personas, creating matching content for each buying stage, and putting this all into our marketing automation platform. This better be best practice! Or even better!

I set out to build my ideal architecture. With nobody to answer to, nobody to convince, I have true carte blanche. I genuinely want everything to come together, to have nurturing, scoring, and everything else all balanced. We have sixteen value propositions. So I create an interest scoring program for each value proposition. Then I create a matching scoring field for each. I create workflows not only on relevant page views and downloads but also on survey answers, keywords in chat conversations, website polls, and videos watched. I look at specific job titles that would be unique for a specific proposition. I also overhaul our preference center to match the sixteen topics. Changes in preferences also count in the interest-scoring programs. I create sixteen different nurture programs, each with three streams to match the three key phases in the buyer's journey. But these nurture programs are not only for generating new business. They are also targeted at existing customers. Each service can have its own buying journey for a customer or prospect. Selling multiple products and/or services can be tricky. Many companies struggle with this. With the help of marketing automation, different marketers and teams can blast their messages to the same recipient. That poor recipient. They can't see the forest for the trees. They're confused by all the messages because they can't see a cohesive story. I expect a lot of people might not agree with me, but I strongly suggest selling one product or service at a time. To have one storyline at a time.

> *"I strongly suggest selling one product or service at a time. To have one storyline at a time."*

I modify the entry criteria for my sixteen nurture programs. A person must have at least a minimum interest score threshold for that topic. But they can't be an active member of another nurture program. How would someone switch from one nurture program to another? Score decay! Whenever an interest score does not increase in a certain timeframe, it's automatically reduced. Whenever it falls below a certain threshold or if the inactivity on the topic lasts too long, the person is set to inactive in that nurture program. This makes the person eligible to enter another nurture program when their interest score is high enough. This results in people going in and out of nurture programs that best meet their interests over time. Someone might be interested in data quality today but then shift focus to video marketing a few months from now.

We're well on our way to creating everything we need for marketing and sales. The other side of the story is the scalability in delivery. A lot of the knowledge is in my head or the heads of colleagues. Formats, templates, and other materials are scattered over customer folders on our shared drive. This makes it difficult to replicate success and best practices.

I start project Wiki. I create sixteen folders, one for every value proposition. In the root are the value proposition document and the factsheet. Each value proposition gets a folder for research and related materials. And it gets a folder with all our internal documentation, customer documentation, build instructions, training materials, and customer work instructions. The documentation does not only include architecture but also the reasoning behind the chosen architecture. All content is written in such a way that any new employee, after proper onboarding, should be able to execute a project at a minimum quality level. It should at least result in a CSAT of eight. It's the skills of a consultant that can make it a nine or ten. It's not about templating the end products, as we believe in real customized work. It's about carefully describing a recipe for success. But still, it's going to be slightly different every time the meal is prepared. Taste and preference change over time. So does the recipe. Every consultant becomes the owner of one or more value propositions to keep their best practices.

> *"Good documentation ensures an eight or better CSAT. It's the commitment of consultant that can boost that to a nine or ten."*

I connect our cloud storage to a custom "Wiki" object in our Salesforce. I then connect the content to the customer and project through the "Product" object in Salesforce. Any employee at Chapman Bright can see which projects are connected to customers and which value propositions connect to the project. One click further, and they can see all the materials for the value proposition. The other way around works as well. When browsing a value proposition, you can also see which customers and projects are associated with that value proposition and how satisfied these customers are with the project.

The most important thing is that everything ties back to the idea that people should not fall into the "Toolbox Trap." It takes a defined goal, a roadmap toward that goal, a methodology, leveraging best practices, testing and scaling hypotheses, and excellence in several fields (technology, data, processes, and change management) to truly achieve success after success.

But what if prospects or customers want to cut corners? What if a company only wants us to do a technical implementation and some training? What if they don't want to define goals? We should ensure that all the customers we accept and all the proposals we write for them should have all the ingredients to become successful. And if we want to cocreate successes with customers, we should no longer accept projects where required ingredients for success are missing. We'll have to do our best to get the proper ingredients for success throughout the sales process. But there comes a time when you must walk out of an RFP process. That's easier said than done.

How do you get those proper ingredients in? It's not just with bigger digital transformation projects or marketing automation implementation projects. It's also with smaller projects. Imagine a customer that wants a new email preference center because they see quite a few unsubscribes. Building, testing, and then going live does not equal success. Implementing technology is not a goal.

"Building, testing, and then going live does not equal success. Implementing technology is not a goal!"

After a few questions, we realized that they did not know the cause of the unsubscribes or how many there were exactly. How would they evaluate the success of the new preference center? We start by setting up a monitoring system to track the mailable percentage of the database (also per source). We then start with the new preference center. But we don't stop there. We also deploy all kinds of other mechanisms to improve the ratio.

We suggest improving their forms. A consent checkbox may not be prechecked for new people in Europe. I did many tests in the past. Did you know that when you add a mandatory question for consent with two radio buttons (yes and no), it drives up the number of people who choose yes? When people want to submit the form, they get an error message stating that they must make a choice. And people who select yes did this consciously. We also propose to leverage transactional emails after form fills. Did a person not consent in the whitepaper download form? Provide a conditional message in the transactional email with the whitepaper download to ask them to subscribe if they like the content. We also propose to involve inside sales and sales. They often speak to people on the phone. There's an opportunity to get people on your consent list. Allow them to send a consent confirmation email from the CRM system. We also propose an evaluation meeting to be held three months after going live to measure and discuss the impact of the project on the mailable database percentage.

"It's often hard for buyers to compare proposals from agencies and vendors. Both mention the same words (e.g. lead scoring), but slight nuances in the details can make or break your success."

We use a similar approach in other projects (e.g., in lead scoring). For buyers, it's often hard to compare proposals from agencies and vendors. Both mention lead scoring on the list of capabilities or statement of work. But the difference can be gigantic. For example, some vendors only offer a single score. And the only setting you have is that you can put in a number for each type of predefined behavior. That might sound sufficient for a small business. But it would be worthless for a larger company. You need to be able to define the behavior in detail. For example, when a lead did not visit the website in the last three months and suddenly has three visits in a single week. And you then want to award a score for the renewed interest. And scoring for multiple products and/or services can only be done with multiple scoring fields. I'm not even going into things like persona scoring or ambassador scoring.

Ambassador Scoring

Who are your true ambassadors? It's pretty similar to determining which leads have the highest propensity to buy. You deploy scoring to score those elements that would be ideal for an ambassador (figure below). And you create a separate lifecycle for ambassadors.

Customer > **Active Customer** >
Potential Ambassador > **Ambassador** > **Top Ambassador**

	Implicit	Explicit
Demographic	E.g., reach. What is the network size on their LinkedIn, Twitter, or Facebook?	E.g., role. Is it an executive or a vice-president?
Behavior	E.g., sentiment. Are they positive, neutral, or negative in their messages about your brand?	E.g., activity. Do they share your content? How often? Reduce scores for periods of inactivity.

A high ambassador score should reflect an individual that is seen as an authority and that is actively sharing positive messages about you to a large audience. When a score threshold is exceeded, the individual is marked as a potential ambassador, like an MQL. The customer marketing team can then reach out to the individual and make it official. The score still helps to distinguish "Ambassadors" from "Top Ambassadors."

Sungevity provides another example of the difference between "scoring" and "scoring." The cost of acquisition is rising in the solar panel business. It's costly to create roof calculations and offers for leads. A part of the created roof calculations never makes it to sales. Different seasonal campaigns can generate more leads than sales can handle in a certain time frame. How can a pool of leads be stored? And how can only the leads with the highest propensity to buy be persuaded to engage and then be handed over to sales at the right time?

Some of the many tested and scaled hypotheses were related to scoring. Scoring doesn't have to be bound to values filled out in forms and/or web behavior. What if we can add more demographic data? If an address corresponds to a rented apartment, chances are pretty slim for buying solar panels for that address. There is so much you can do to improve scoring algorithms (e.g., with data appending and/or intent data).

Best practices, a BHAG, great colleagues, customers, a brand, marketing materials, and now value propositions—they're all ready. It's time to lay the last piece of the puzzle and finalize my methodology.

Sungevity
Customer Story

This Chapter's Challenges	This Chapter's Solutions
How to engage C-level executives (CEO and CSO) on the topic of marketing automation? How to convince them it's the right investment (ROI).	The most important is to not fall into the "Toolbox Trap." It takes a defined goal, a roadmap toward that goal, a methodology, leveraging best practices, testing and scaling hypotheses, and excellence in several fields (technology, data, processes, and change management) to truly achieve success after success.
How to (internally) sell your recipes for success?	Create a value proposition document for your ideas. What key questions does your idea answer? What's the value?
How can you nurture prospects for different products and services over time?	Use a scoring field and scoring algorithm per proposition. Nurture prospects about one service at a time, starting with the service that currently has the highest interest and engagement.
What can you do to replicate success?	Productize your knowledge. Use a Wiki. Integrate it into your onboarding process.
How to ensure the ingredients for success are there?	Try to convince your customer or leadership to think beyond technical implementation. And if they won't budge? Don't do the project!

How to go beyond just a technical implementation to ensure success (e.g., with setting up email preferences)?	Monitor the health of your preferences. Create a benchmark to start from. Improve processes, such as consent radio buttons for forms and the use of transactional emails. And measure the impact of each of these sources.
How to compare MarTech features and services?	Have an innovation budget next to default implementation steps.
How can you leverage scoring techniques to detect your potential ambassadors and top ambassadors?	A high ambassador score should reflect an individual that is seen as an authority and that is actively sharing positive messages about you to a large audience.
What can you use in scoring beyond values filled out in forms and/or web behavior?	Data appending with demographics. Or intent data.

CHAPLOOP™:
A MODEL TO GROW YOUR BUSINESS THROUGH MARTECH

Everything is coming together: how to replicate successes, when marketing automation doesn't work, and what the crucial ingredients for success are. I take my methodology to the next level, and I name it. I even trademark it.

Nowadays, your prospects and customers expect your company to stay relevant by understanding them. Ever-improving and more-affordable marketing technology allows your company, and your competitors, to do just that. It's up to you to win the race against your competition.

The Chaploop™ methodology enables you to consistently grow your business through MarTech. Your company's marketing technology stack is like a growth hacker's toolbox to test new marketing and sales ideas and then scale those ideas that work.

A big issue with MarTech implementations today is that people think of MarTech as a big magic button that solves their challenges upon installation. But once you have unpacked your growth hacker's toolbox, you'll need to (know how to) leverage it. The second big issue is that companies still treat some marketing technologies as channels (e.g., Marketo as just a campaign platform or even just for emails). With the Chaploop™, there is a repeatable methodology that puts all the pieces and topics together in a meaningful way.

CHAPLOOP **GROWING YOUR BUSINESS WITH**

LEAD MANAGEMENT
ACCOUNT BASED MARKETING
SALES ENABLEMENT
SERVICE LEVEL AGREEMENTS

CENTER OF EXCELLENCE
(DE)CENTRALIZATION

CHAPMAN BRIGHT
MARTECH FANATICS

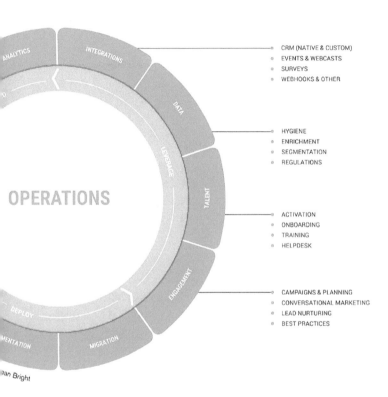

- CRM (NATIVE & CUSTOM)
- EVENTS & WEBCASTS
- SURVEYS
- WEBHOOKS & OTHER

- HYGIENE
- ENRICHMENT
- SEGMENTATION
- REGULATIONS

- ACTIVATION
- ONBOARDING
- TRAINING
- HELPDESK

- CAMPAIGNS & PLANNING
- CONVERSATIONAL MARKETING
- LEAD NURTURING
- BEST PRACTICES

an Bright

Strategy > Discover

<u>Strategy > Discover > Accelerate</u>

Looking at success stories in the market and growth stories from our customers, I found that acceleration and repeatable growth through marketing and sales typically start with a hypothesis, an idea, likely based on an assessment. This could be a simple idea, such as the hypothesis that having inside sales cold call leads or call low-quality leads is too costly. And that calling warm, more nurtured leads could reduce the cost of customer acquisition (and improve the employee satisfaction of inside sales representatives).

Tying your digital transformation to such hypotheses/growth potential scenarios gives you a much better chance of reaching your goals compared to the alternative. The alternative is the "Toolbox Trap," where you focus on delivering new capabilities and train your staff on the new tools. That by itself will not result in transformation. You must understand that there is a difference between change and transformation!

<u>Strategy > Discover > Assessments</u>

Discovering your growth potential starts with an assessment, interviewing stakeholders from different parts of the business to discover the different hypotheses for growth and improvement. Plot and prioritize the ideas based on effort and impact. Then work your way around the loop. First as a small pilot, and then scale those ideas that work.

Strategy > Marketing & Sales Strategy

Change always impacts the organization and requires proper strategy. How do you design your company's organization for repeatable and scalable success? How do you align your marketing and sales?

Will your management of your MarTech be centralized, decentralized, or hybrid? It all depends on politics or where the talent is in your company. Which department and/or roles should get which responsibilities after you've deployed your MarTech? And what are the best practices to leverage to align your marketing and sales?

Strategy > M&S Strategy > Organizational Design

Seventy percent of digital transformations do not reach the desired results. Companies fail to understand the difference between change and transformation. And companies often fall into the "Toolbox Trap." Implementing new technology, even when combined with user training, is not sufficient. You must organize for success and leverage best practices.

Strategy > M&S Strategy > Sales Enablement

Sales and marketing too often find themselves being the stereotypes they are. Sales is traditional and has no need or desire to chance. Marketing is enthusiastic and eager to change and leverage new technologies. On many occasions, marketing pushes digital change with minimal or no involvement from sales. This is not ideal, but it's better than doing nothing as digital change is necessary, even when sales doesn't realize it. The world is changing into a place where you constantly need to adapt to changing digital environments and buying behavior.

Aligning marketing and sales is mission critical in this new world. Marketing technology and sales technology can help bridge the gap, but they are not the solution. Though sales enablement tools do often result in small successes that gradually build trust between both disciplines.

Strategy > Prepare

Once you are organized to improve, you will have to determine your business case and define appropriate pilots. How will you get the most out of your investments? How to work agilely in projects, with small steps toward success? Which benchmarks can you use in your business case to make sure it is as realistic as possible? How to write a project initiation document (PID) if you have never implemented relevant MarTech before? How to avoid pitfalls and ensure best practices? Which disciplines and experts should be included on your project teams?

Strategy > Prepare > Business Case

Marketers tend to surround themselves with the latest technologies and innovations. It's easy for them to fall into the trap of constantly implementing new technologies without proper business case justification.

Every loop through the Chaploop™ starts with a hypothesis for growth. A "mini-case" is worked out, and a pilot is started. Tools are semi-implemented, leveraged, and then assessed for their contribution to business value. Those ideas that work and create value are scaled up but not before another round of creating a new and bigger business case. After that, a more scalable implementation follows. Tools are being levered and validated again and again for their contribution to business value creation.

Strategy > Prepare > Pilots

Try, try, try! When you take more steps than you fall, you're moving forward. You're innovating. Though you should minimize the times you fail to innovate faster, not taking any steps at all will prevent you from ever innovating. Accept failure and try. Create a company climate where it's okay to try and fail. That's why pilots are so important for innovation and creating business value. Implement at a small scale with limited resources and learn. Then scale those pilots that work and are promising. The outcome of a pilot is as good as its preparation. A successful pilot comes from standardization and a structured approach. Leverage your best-practice pilot templates for repeatable success.

Strategy > Prepare > Projects

After your hypothesis, you work out the business case and pilot definition. But before you implement, you must take a step back and properly define the project. The better prepared you are, the more likely you are to succeed!

How do you write a project initiation document (PID) if you have never implemented similar MarTech before? How can you avoid common pitfalls, and how can you make sure to leverage the latest best practices? Which disciplines and experts should be included on your project teams? Answer these and many other preparation questions before you start your implementation phase.

Operations > Deploy

How can you deploy MarTech with best practices from the start? How to avoid pitfalls? Have you thought about migrating your old ways to the new platforms? Make sure you tailor your implementation to your company's unique needs. Have you also thought about data and integrations? A problem I often see is that companies unpack the box but forget to leverage their efforts. Another common mistake is forgetting about people. It's not about the technology but what you can do with it. Fifty percent is change management. Don't forget to leverage your talent.

Operations > Deploy > Implementation

You've worked out your hypothesis for growth; you've prepared (e.g., pilot, business case); and now you're ready to implement.

Operations > Deploy > Migration

People tend to forget that when you implement a new marketing technology, you are often migrating from a previous platform. Or at least from a related technology that will sunset.

You will have to migrate and transform your data. You must train staff and update processes and ways of working. Or in some scenarios, you're refreshing and/or reinstalling a marketing technology. No matter the reason for migrating, you'll be facing some challenges. Lessons from several migration projects resulted in a method that takes several things into account (e.g., team activation, a scalable process for migrating campaigns, contacts, and data, but also keeping your business alive while migrating).

Operations > Leverage

After you've implemented your new marketing technology and related processes and migrated from your old ways, the real work starts. You can only grow when you build on top of previous successes and failures. A lot of companies fall into what I call a "postimplementation black hole." Everybody has worked so hard to go live that they need a well-deserved break. That's when the momentum is lost, and putting new technology to use goes into a freefall. Don't let your investment go to waste!

Operations > Leverage > Engagement

How can you ensure that you can leverage what you have deployed? One of the crucial factors is engagement. Everything you do evolves around your (potential) customer. How can you optimally leverage your engagement with them through nurturing, scoring, events, webinars, chat, feedback, or conversational marketing? How can you leverage lessons and best practices with a center of excellence and templated campaigns?

Operations > Leverage > Talent

Leveraging your staff is crucial for successfully adding business value from your marketing technology. Activate your staff after going live to avoid falling into the postimplementation black hole. You also need to make sure to document your decisions so you can build on them in the future. A lot of companies train their staff at the time of implementation, but what about your future new staff? You need work instructions, on-demand training materials, and period-recurring (onboarding) training, preferably with in-company certification. Second, 50% of business success comes from change management. So next to training, you also have to think about other ways for your staff to adopt the new ways. And until you have gained the minimum level of experience, you can build on external experts to guide you through your journey of growth.

Operations > Leverage > Data

Garbage in means garbage out. Hopefully, you'll have heard that quote many times before. It's a bit of an open door, but you'll be surprised how many companies have not budgeted for data within their implementation and/or migration of marketing technology. You've significantly invested in marketing technology, but data is essential for generating business value. As with leveraging your staff, you should also leverage your data to drive business value.

What's the cost of bad data (e.g., poor campaign results, poor reporting, and/or not adhering to data regulations)? Ensure your processes prevent bad data from the start. And think about the possibilities of consistently increasing and enriching your database to drive business value.

Operations > Leverage > Integrations

Similar to your engagement, talent, and data, your marketing technology will drive so much more business value when you can leverage integrations. Your marketing automation platform and your CRM could be considered the left and right chambers of the heart of your commercial business. Together, they create synergy to supercharge your business.

Another example could be determining interest by leveraging the data on how customers engage with your videos from your video marketing platform. This interest profile could then be made available to the account manager in CRM to make sure he or she is having the right discussions at the next customer meeting.

Operations > Business Value Added

Looking at success stories in the market and growth stories from my projects, I found that repeatable growth through marketing and sales typically starts with a hypothesis. Hypotheses come from insights, not from reports, analytics, or tables. Understanding what makes your business grow through MarTech does not come from a simplistic dashboard. If you're doing well, you'll have metrics available for data-driven decisions.

Operations > Business Value Added > BI & Analytics

First, you had a hypothesis for which you implemented your (new) marketing technologies. And now you've leveraged those technologies. But you want to know how it performs. Is it working? You need to define the metrics to track performance. But even more important, you want to be able to change course. You want to be in the driver's seat in order to impact the outcome. Defining the different levels of metrics is key.

Operations > Business Value Added > Success Management

Success management is not the same as analytics. It's not dashboards, reports, and metrics. What most people think about is reporting on the performance of activities and/or processes. But those that have gone a step further and formulated proper KPIs that allow them not only to measure performance but also impact the outcome—they are in the driver's seat. But all of that is still looking at performance (and for some, being able to impact that performance).

Success management is about evaluating how each loop in the Chaploop™, from hypothesis to execution, contributes to creating business value. That helps you gain new insights to take the next loop, creating a continuous cycle of business value generating innovation through marketing and sales technology, which is embedded within the organization.

Let's say you've grown from traditional marketing to modern marketing. You've invested time, money, resources, and more to implement marketing automation. Your organization is now talking about MQLs, and you can even steer and impact the number of MQLs. But did this entire journey create business value? How should you evaluate this? That's what success management is all about.

"Maybe in a next book I can provide you with more in-depth cases, examples, templates, and formats to help you operationalize Chaploop™ at your business."

Chaploop™
Website

Fortunately, according to Gartner, businesses will invest more in innovation and methods to remain competitive. I hope they also invest in creating a company climate that enourages trying and failing because that's going to be their biggest leap forward, not the technology itself.

"Close to two-thirds (63%) of CMOs will be increasing their innovation budgets in 2019 as they 'embrace new channels, models and methods to remain competitive.'"

Gartner

At Chapman Bright, I now have everything I need (value propositions, our Wiki, and a proven methodology). I significantly invested in a new brand, including a new website, events, and video. We hired two more colleagues to join the team in late 2019. And I also invested in a big new office. It nearly depletes our cash reserves. But business is picking up. All lights are green.

Surely 2020 is going to be great . . .

This Chapter's Challenges	This Chapter's Solutions
Is there a recipe, a methodology, or a way of working to drive business growth through MarTech?	Use all the steps in both wheels of the Chaploop™ for a continuous cycle of business value generating innovation through marketing and sales technology, embedded within your organization.

BONUS: DIGITAL ACCELERATION IN A PANDEMIC

Then I Realized What Was About to Happen as of March 2020

Fast forward to one year later. It's April 2021. I'm alone in a cottage at a holiday park to complete the final chapters of this book. I originally planned to write about the period between late 2009 and early 2020, a time span of about ten years. Six of the original thirteen chapters are already completed. I wrote them in the summer of 2020 during the COVID-19 pandemic. A drop in consulting hours at the end of the first wave freed up time to write. That same first wave impacted my growth plans for Chapman Bright. So I decided to add an extra chapter to this book to share my experiences with digital acceleration in a pandemic.

It's March 3, 2020. I'm in Paris for business when I hear the Adobe Summit in the United States was canceled. Adobe is among the first the cancel their events even though there were hardly any COVID-19 cases in the United States at the time. It's Friday, March 13, when we get a call from Niels van den Brink at our partner Eisenfelt. He shares the great news that he received a verbal agreement from his customer to start a new project together. The kick-off meeting will be on Tuesday. The kick-off meeting would also be a festive moment to sign the paperwork in person. It's Sunday when the Dutch government holds a press conference. COVID-19 cases are rapidly increasing after the winter holidays and the Dutch carnival, rising from about 50 to 250 confirmed infections nationwide per day. While surrounding countries go into full lockdown, we go into smart lockdown. But panic and fear still set in. It's Monday, and we hear that the kick-off meeting on Tuesday is canceled. The company specializes in the placement of expats. And all expats are flying home. COVID-19 will likely hit them hard. With all the uncertainties, they stop all investments. A few days later, I learn that an enterprise customer of ours will not extend our contract for the second quarter as they have no idea if and how the pandemic will impact their business. That same day, Arjen mentions another enterprise customer is shredding all contracts with external suppliers, as their revenue will likely drop by more than 90%. Luckily, our work there was invoiced in advance. We still have months of work contracted. So we should be fine for a while. Though I notice that we haven't received a single new online lead in the system for days now. And it stays that way until we get our first new lead in the second week of May nearly eight weeks later.

We're still working on existing contracts throughout those eight weeks. I calculate that we'll see a decline in work as of mid-May. It looks like it will be a long slow summer! A few slow months shouldn't be problematic under normal circumstances.

I find out there are many ways to tackle a crisis (e.g., introduce channel or licensing models, adjust pricing models). According to Simon-Kucher & Partners, there are six areas to focus on:

- Adjust cost and plan for multiple scenarios (e.g., reduce full-time staff, starting with low-performers, introduce contractors)
- Stay close to your customers and protect revenue (e.g., double down on your key accounts that drive most revenue)
- Implement smart pricing and protect margins (e.g., defend prices and offer less expensive alternatives)
- Revise commercial model and realign sources (e.g., adjust your offering to focus on services that still provide value)
- Capitalize on growth areas (e.g., which products and core markets still have growth potential?)
- Prepare for eventual rebound (e.g., assess competitive moves and develop responses, or buy up competition)

But let's zoom in on some more tangible digital initiatives you could take and prepare for.

What If Market Demand Drops for Your Products and/or Services?

Then you can still grow, but you will have to do it at the expense of your competition. Be quicker to respond. Be better at addressing the needs of your prospects. Better understand your audience in order to be more relevant than your competition. You can put more effort into your differentiating products/services with higher margins to take more market share. But you can also increase your market share by being better in the digital game than your competition.

Increase your capability to drive more net new names. Use new and innovative digital methods to convert leads. Offer your website visitors more and different ways to convert. Some examples include chat and conversational marketing to enable leads to book meetings with sales straight away. Or you can migrate your videos from YouTube/Vimeo to an actual professional video platform, which enables you to add forms throughout your videos. Perhaps highly target your content on LinkedIn and leverage the LinkedIn Lead Gen Form functionality. Also, make sure you follow up on your leads more quickly than the competition!

What If Your Cost per Deal Is Too High to Compete?

You can reduce your cost of acquisition with your online marketing spending on ads, but you can also improve sales alignment and your lead management process. Doubling up on digital can also result in new channels and methods to drive cheaper leads at scale. You could beat your competitors by making sure your cost of acquisition is lower than your competitors'. Lowering or optimizing your ad spend is something you've likely already covered. But don't waste those expensively generated leads. Make sure your lead management process is state of the art. SiriusDecisions found that companies that have excellent lead management processes get eight times more business out of the same number of new names than companies that do not properly manage their lead management process. So there is so much room for improvement. Integrate your marketing automation platform with your CRM in a proper way. Date-stamp your lead stages. Have clear SLAs between marketing and sales. Ensure a swift lead follow-up. Leverage sales enablement tools. Structurally communicate between marketing and sales. All this enables you to maintain your sales velocity and shorten the sales cycle and increase the lead-to-business ratio.

On top of those digital initiatives, you could double down on existing deals in the pipeline. This is especially important for B2B companies with a complex long sales cycle. Companies with a short transactional sales cycle could fully focus on new name generation.

What If You've Luckily Come Up with New Anticyclic Products or Services, But Are Not Able to Launch Them Quickly Enough?

Your marketing technology stack should be set up in such a way, with supporting processes and organizational skills, that you can always test, launch, and scale new initiatives at lightning speed. One way to thrive during a recession is by introducing new products and/or services that fit the new reality. And when you create those after some investment, it's key to be able to go to market at speed.

If you have done your job proficiently, you should have a marketing technology stack and organization that are flexible and scalable. Your MarTech should be your growth hacker's dream toolbox to quickly test and pilot new hypotheses and then scale those ideas that work. Adding new campaigns, new nurture streams, new content, new channels, and/or new products should take you minimal effort. Double up on digital now to ensure your MarTech stack is robust enough for challenges or opportunities in the near future.

What If Your Prospects and Customers Become Reluctant to Invest in Larger Commitments? How Can You Help Them Overcome This?

Demand will also drop within your current customer base (and existing prospect list). How can you gain trust and nurture them to still purchase your products and/or services? But also make sure to double up in your key accounts!

It's important to double down on your key accounts by understanding their pains and addressing them (e.g., overdeliver on service, update payment terms, collaborate with them). For midvalue customers, focus on specific business opportunities only. And make sure to increase the average deal size by upselling where possible. But prepare yourself for prospects and customers that will become reluctant to invest (large sums) in your products or services. Yes, you can offer them price alternatives, but the price is not the issue. Your customers and prospects must be able to value your products and service to justify the price tag. So you must educate them! Lead nurturing is now more important than ever. Even if they don't buy now due to budget issues, they might buy after the recession!

After a peak of about 1,250 confirmed infections per day, numbers drop to about fifty per day by the end of May. Life returns to a "new normal" in the Netherlands. We sign a contract renewal for the third quarter with the customer that skipped the second quarter. We also start seeing new leads coming in again. This should drive the first new contracts in four to ten weeks from now. One of those new leads is Bial, a midsize research-based international pharmaceutical company headquartered in Portugal. Their core strength is development and innovation for central nervous system diseases. Their ambition is to achieve a level of digital excellence that will allow them to compete with other players in this field. Their core audience consists of health care professionals (HCPs). There's a gap between traditional pharma engagement methods and the current needs of HCPs. They are looking for a methodology to gain momentum in their commercial digital transformation.

Together with the team at Bial, we made the following steps to gain momentum in their transformation:

- Compile a broad perspective on the current and desired states of digital customer engagement through interviews. What are the common threats and opportunities? Assess the use of the current technologies. Assess the skills and competencies of people.
- Based on that, define the organizational and technical capabilities required to get to the desired state.
- Look at complexity versus urgency to identify and prioritize the different phases to close the gap. Create a detailed roadmap for each phase and ensure quick wins are achieved early in parallel.

In parallel, apply methods that energize the stakeholders to gradually gain that digital transformation momentum. Make sure people are heard and that they can contribute.

Bial
Customer Story

After the summer, we're finishing up the project at Bial, and it seems like everybody in Europe is accelerating their digital initiatives, as traditional methods no longer work. Demand is increasing. I see an uptick in business and the number of new leads. Is this just a rebound after the slow months before the summer? Is demand structurally rising? Should I further grow the business? Should I hire new colleagues to work on the additional projects? The pipeline looks good, but it seems somewhat risky at this point.

I reflect and think about all the work and investment in the past years throughout the fall of 2020. The most important finding is that our customer satisfaction keeps rising. We went from an eight out of ten average to an average of nine out of ten. That's the proof and foundation that I was looking for. The last months have been steady, so Jacques and I pull the trigger and hire Ellen Schwier and Bas van Buuren. Both will start in the first weeks of 2021. It's our BHAG "Guiding Success Stories" that drive the increase in satisfaction. They result in more renewals and a higher customer lifetime value. How did we achieve this?

I see many companies running their satisfaction surveys about once per year and at an arbitrary date. It's like sticking a thermometer in a frying pan and judging if the temperature of the oil is to your liking. It says absolutely nothing about the core temperature of the food in the frying pan. Or if it's ready or not. Or if it's crispy. Or even how it will taste.

> *"How would you feel if you provided feedback but never heard anything back about it?"*

An annual satisfaction survey will only allow you to improve your processes once per year. And it could take months to find out a customer is dissatisfied and then engage that customer in real-time to turn things around. A better way would be to leverage feedback throughout the lifecycle. And marketing automation plays a key role in enabling you to do that.

Outtakes from My Different Keynotes on Leveraging Customer Feedback:

- Leverage custom objects and activities in your marketing automation platform (e.g., winning an opportunity, closing a helpdesk ticket, attending an event, starting, or completing a project, etc.) Use these activities to trigger survey emails.

- Connect these emails to your integrated survey platform for the data to flow back into the customer's profile. Or link to a landing page with a form in your marketing automation platform.

- Create different CSAT fields for each key milestone in the customer journey. That way, you can get insights into where in the process you do well or not (e.g., after signing the first deal, completing a project, annual renewal, etc.).

- You can even directly ask a question in the email itself. Clicking on an answer could directly prepopulate the form.

- Connect the CSAT fields to your CRM so that sales and service can also see how satisfied each individual is.

- Create workflows to create tasks for the activity owners to follow up on low satisfaction scores. This enables you to directly act and get back to your customers to turn things around.

- Group individual satisfaction scores on the company level to determine the level of satisfaction of the entire company. For example, you can use the last individual's satisfaction score or a three-month running average of all individual scores.

Watch my Adobe
Summit presentation
on how to leverage
Marketo for this.

Understanding your audience is vital to being relevant to them. It helps you to beat the competition. That becomes even more important in a pandemic or economic crisis. Interest scoring can be combined with matching nurture programs to drive cohesive and relevant engagement over time. But what more can we do to understand even better—to further improve scoring algorithms?

Tracking Page Views versus Tracking Page Interaction Weight

A marketing automation platform typically comes with a tracking JavaScript to include in your website's template. It creates a cookie for visitors. It can connect the visitor to a record in the database (e.g., after a form fill or clicked link in an email). The tracking script then registers each visited page to the lead's activity history. It also tracks each clicked link on those pages. This allows you to create a variety of workflows (e.g., increase interest score for a solution if the lead visits one or more pages on the website around that same solution). But what does a page view say about intent? Is it a short page or a page with a lot of content? Did they spend five seconds on the page or five minutes? Did they scroll down? Which paragraphs did they read? Write custom code to enhance your tracking script to weight the page view. For example, a score from one to ten that weights the height of the page, how long someone was on the page, and how far they scrolled. Then inject that into your tracking code right before they leave the page.

Tracking Whitepaper Downloads versus Whitepaper Consumption

I do not know anyone with a marketing automation platform without some content on their website to download. Sometimes this content is behind a form (gated). But often it is also ungated. On many occasions, it drives the lead to a PDF (e.g., whitepaper). A PDF is a file, and there's no tracking script. So you can only see that they clicked through to the PDF. I bet that your scoring algorithm awards some points for clicking through to that whitepaper. But what does that mean? A better method would be to create a tracked landing page to embed the PDF on. And point the lead to the embedded PDF rather than to the PDF itself. But that still has some limitations. Yes, your advanced page-tracking script could detect how many seconds they were on the page, but it can't detect the size of the PDF. Use a document cloud plugin (e.g., Adobe's Document Cloud PDF Software Development Kit). Create some custom code for your tracking script to log each viewed PDF page as a separate pageview.

Marketo once provided me with a Marketo Engage developers sandbox for developing and testing software, such as CalcItnow. Partner agencies are normally provided with a services sandbox to showcase capabilities to prospects. But one sandbox was enough for me. Marketo was so kind as to manually adjust my developer's sandbox to make it look like a services sandbox after I pulled the plug on my software endeavor. But the former developer's sandbox does have some challenges (e.g., Adobe's new UI can't be easily applied). So we too migrate to a new and fresh Marketo Engage environment. A regionally hosted new services sandbox. So we refrain from really sending a significant amount of production emails to customers. We send a few, especially around our Adobe-sponsored events. We do need some data to showcase the capabilities of Marketo Engage to customers. And I want to be able to show a real environment with real data. I don't wait to showcase a fake environment with messed-up dummy data. It just makes me sad to see sales from software companies demonstrate fake setups. Where is the "practice what you preach" mentality?

With our new instance and our capabilities to better understand enable higher relevance, I think about more ways to be relevant. I want to make advancements in personalization.

Content Suggestions by Artificial Intelligence (AI)

We suggest related content on most pages of our website. But they are all static. They are added manually when creating the page. With a few hundred web pages, it's cumbersome to constantly update the related content section on every page whenever new content is published. The same applies to our confirmation page, the page you see after submitting a form. Inspired by earlier work for customers and by the presentation of a customer at our 2019 event in London, we activate the predictive content module in our Marketo Engage instance.

The predictive content module automatically learns and categorizes content on our website. It also learns to predict which content might likely resonate with similar visitors. I can now place a piece of custom code on our website to generate a section with three AI-suggested pieces of content. I now must wait for the developers to create a custom page component for our CMS to easily add the section to a page rather than mess with raw code and CSS styling. Jampacked with customer projects, I'm hoping for this to go live in the spring of 2021.

Web Personalization

Another way to be more relevant is to personalize your corporate website in real-time. Ideally, you would use a personalization platform that is either connected to or part of your marketing automation platform. It will allow you to leverage the lead properties and segments to personalize. For example, you can target customers with a different call to action (CTA) than a potential employee or prospect.

Chat Playbooks and Conversational Pages

The same applies to conversational marketing like chat or conversational landing pages. Chat platforms that have both back-end integration and front-end integration can detect the identity of the visitor. Needless to say, this will drive better and more meaningful conversations. Help your visitor answer their questions. Let them directly schedule meetings with your support or sales representatives. Or even let these colleagues take over the automated conversations. You can even consider removing forms and ungating your content. Instead, you can have a meaningful automated conversation through chat based on the exact page the person is reading in the whitepaper.

Download the slides from
Planon's Road To
Predictive Personalization

It's early December 2020. The team and I have been working hard to support our customers. It's been so busy I haven't written a single chapter for this book since my summer holiday in France in 2020. But I have some personal time off planned for January 2021 to continue with this book. It seems like the only way to block out the time to continue writing. I really want my experiences on paper for others to benefit from.

Then mid-December, even with all the precautions, I start to feel weak, and I lose my sense of smell. I get tested for COVID-19 later that day. But I already know what they'll find. I already go in complete isolation on our attic. The next morning, I receive the call that I tested positive. I experience the first few days worse than an average flu. Nothing to worry about. That changes on the fourth day. I quickly become shorter and shorter of breath, and I start to get nervous. I call my general practitioner the next morning, and he tells me: "As long as you're not crawling on the floor, thinking you're about to pass out, there's nothing to worry about . . . yet." Luckily, my shortness of breath goes away that day as quickly as it emerged the day before.

I realize that I'm lucky. A year earlier, I realized that I neglected my health for the entire duration of my entrepreneurship since late 2015. I made some serious lifestyle changes in 2020, eating healthier, walking at least five miles twice a week, and hitting the gym at least two to three times per week (whenever it wasn't closed due to the pandemic of course). Just in time, I transformed from being in the COVID-19 high-risk category to being able to fight it off.

The day before I can leave isolation, I feel much better. Being away from work eased my mind, and I open my notebook. I start to write the next chapter "How to Achieve Award-Worthy ROI." It takes me over ten hours to complete just a few pages. They'll probably require quite a bit of editing afterward.

But when will I be able to finish the book? What are the next steps for Chapman Bright? We still have a backlog of over sixty project case studies to write. But most importantly, what will the next five to ten years bring?

This Chapter's Challenges	This Chapter's Solutions
Which digital steps can you take to win during an economic crisis, when market demand drops for your products and/or services?	Better understand and be more relevant to your audience than your competition. Master your lead management process to avoid leads falling through the cracks. Leverage automation and nurturing to educate your audience about the value of your services.
How to gain momentum in digital transformation?	Compile a broad perspective on the current and desired states of digital customer engagement through interviews. Close the organizational and technical gap with a phased roadmap and deliver quick wins in parallel.
How to leverage feedback throughout the lifecycle?	Create workflows around custom objects and activities at key lifecycle milestones and create tasks to directly improve satisfaction in real-time.
How to improve scoring algorithms for web behavior?	Use custom scripts to improve the tracking scripts to include the weight of the page view (e.g., time versus page length and scrolling). Use custom scripts and document clouds to track individual PDF pageviews.
How to be ever more relevant to your audiences?	Suggest interesting content through machine learning. Personalize your website in real-time. Leverage chat and conversational landing pages.

MARTECH BEYOND ~~2020~~ 2021

This book now spans about eleven years rather than ten years due to the bonus chapter on "Digital Acceleration in a Pandemic." But I also would like to share my thoughts on the next five to ten years. What are my predictions for the market? What are my hopes? And how will it impact me?

I described an acceleration in digital after the summer of 2020. I also described that it wasn't a temporary catch-up but that it looks structural. I'm not the only one noticing this. Digital is the new normal. The COVID-19 pandemic increased the acceptance of more digital into the lives of people. Even before the start of the pandemic, it was the global chairman Tamara Ingra from Wunderman Thompson that said on ThinkWithGoogle:

> "By the year 2030, what is really exciting is most things will be frictionless. Everything will be purchasable. Everything will turn from product to service. So I think we're looking at a way of really helping people in their lives."

Tamara Ingra

As a result, I think that mobile will no longer be one of the marketing channels, but it will be at its center (e.g., walking into a store, grabbing products, and walking out without having to pay at the cashier).

Speaking of channels, I also hope we bury disputes around lead sources and stop mixing channels, lead sources, campaigns, and initiatives as values in the "Lead Source" field. We need to make sure our data is of a high quality. Like Adam New-Waterson posted on LinkedIn: "Repeat after me. Demo request is not a lead source."

We're able to make better and better data-driven decisions. But like I already presented in 2019, I see that marketing will also be shifting toward a more humanistic purpose. Companies need to develop more empathy. Customers want to be seen and heard. Having a personalized experience is far more effective at creating a memorable and positive experience. How can you shift from servicing to helping customers in their lives? Buying journeys become more and more driven by self-service trials, freemium experiences, and/or subscriptions (e.g., Volvo's car subscription model). This could result in a shift in companies that leans more toward customer experience than marketing.

Alexa who? Humanistic and conversational methods will also drive even more adoption to a new world of search using voice. One of the most discussed and successful pieces of tech to surface in previous years has been voice assistants. But what concerns are there with security and data privacy? Artificial intelligence (AI) is already widely adapted into many marketing strategies (e.g., predictive content and predictive audiences for Marketo Engage or Sensei by Adobe). But until now, AI is siloed and limited to point solutions. I'm not expecting any overarching AI before 2025. But maybe we might be able to leverage unsiloed AI by 2030?

Artificial Intelligence is not the only technology that we'll further adopt in our lives and thus in marketing. The MarTech Landscape by Scott Brinker has progressively grown to 6,800 in 2018. It seems to flatten out a bit to 8,000 in 2020. Will the growth further flatten? Is pretty much everything invented by now? In today's world, change is happening faster every year. And every chance offers new possibilities and innovations. So we'll see many new MarTech solutions rise to the top.

The main challenge is managing your growing MarTech stack. How will you integrate everything? How agile will you be? Like Bial, the pharmaceutical company, you should create a vision for the near future and keep looking forward. Create a phased road map for the next few years. And constantly update it with a new future phase.

But while adopting all these new technologies, what will you be doing to keep up with the growing need for a skilled workforce? And is it sustainable to constantly retrain your staff in these new technologies?

Social media started to become an integral part of our lives around 2005. The like button radically changed culture. Everybody is voicing their opinions, good and bad. We all raise our voices in striving to be an all-inclusive society. But I see more and more people apply self-censorship as they become afraid of the possible opinions of others. Will we become a boring, monotone, and colorless society due to our fear of the opinions of others? Will we achieve the exact opposite of what we intended? Or will the large majority step up and do something about digital bullying? It's not limited to just the general public and governments. Companies can no longer stand on the sideline. They must step up and join the conversation. People will expect companies to contribute to society, to the environment, and in ways that make lives better.

> *"Companies can no longer stand on the sideline. They must step up and join the conversation. People will expect companies to contribute to society, to the environment, and in ways that make lives better."*

Maybe we'll have about fifteen colleagues at Chapman Bright by 2025. And we'll have more customers and projects to contribute to with even more best practices. A growing team will allow me to spend my time contributing in other ways than just in our projects.

Perhaps, building on top of this book, I can again spend more time on presenting more lessons and experiences in keynotes to help even more people and companies succeed.

It's hard to predict the future. But everything will work out just fine, as long I stay true to what I value most. And that is helping others succeed by "guiding success stories."

EPILOGUE

I want to thank you for making it all the way through to this chapter. I genuinely hope there were many things that might help you to succeed in your endeavors. If you have any questions, feel free to connect and reach out to me online (e.g., through LinkedIn). I'll do my best to answer as many questions as possible.

I wrote about my passion for helping others succeed and creating value. I challenge you to do the same. I hope you also want to help others succeed. So recommend this book if you think it could help others succeed too. Pay it forward. Share the link to the book website below on your social channels. Or donate this book to a colleague or friend.

Book
Website

ABOUT THE AUTHOR

Diederik Martens, founder of Chapman Bright and author of the book "Marketing Automation Untangled", is a frequently asked speaker on what it takes to successfully transform marketing, align with sales, and innovate with marketing technology.

Diederik was awarded the international Killer Content Award for his lead nurture campaign strategy at Quintiq. And he was named to the Adobe's world's top-50 in his field multiple times.

Diederik works on marketing transformation projects for companies, mostly in B2B, such as DHL, Deloitte, Trend Micro, Lely, Essent, Staples, Innogy, BDO, Rockwool, PinkRoccade, Dassault Systèmes, Thyssenkrupp, Sungevity, Portbase, Wolf Oil, and many more.

Keynote Speaker
for your event?

MarTech Consultancy
for your company?

Want to connect with
Diederik on LinkedIn?

APPENDIX I:
QUICK GUIDE TO MARKETING

"Marketing refers to activities a company undertakes to promote the buying or selling of a product, service, or good. It is one of the primary components of business management and commerce. Marketers can direct their product to other businesses (B2B marketing) or directly to consumers (B2C marketing)."

Wikipedia.org

"In 1980, I defined marketing as 'satisfying needs and wants through an exchange process', but in 2018 defined it as 'the process by which companies engage customers, build strong customer relationships, and create customer value in order to capture value from customers in return.'"

Philip Kotler

"This discipline centers on the study of market and consumer behaviors and it analyzes the commercial management of companies in order to attract, acquire, and retain customers by satisfying their wants and needs and instilling brand loyalty."

Cyberclick.net

APPENDIX II:
MARKETING AUTOMATION RESOURCES

DiederikMartens.com

ChapmanBright.com

MarketingAutomation
Untangled.com

Marketo Resources

Adobe Resources

Salesforce Resources

Hubspot Resources

Oracle Resources

Sitecore Resources

Marketing Automation
Software: G2

Marketing Automation
Software: TrustRadius

Scott Brinker's
ChiefMarTech

APPENDIX III:
THE 333 DIGITAL MARKETING
& SALES GLOSSARY OF TERMS

If you're in marketing automation, you should have business acumen - *Keenness and quickness in understanding and dealing with a "business situation", such as risks and opportunities, in a manner that is likely to lead to a good outcome.*

You should be proficient in marketing terminology, sales jargon, commerce terms, project management methods, and web development terminology. Please find an extensive list below, that I have compiled over time. Feel free to reach out to me to further complete the list.

301
According to MOZ: "A redirect is a way to send both users and search engines to a different URL from the one they originally requested. The three most commonly used redirects are 301, 302, and Meta Refresh. 301, "Moved Permanently" is recommended for SEO."

404
According to BusinessInsider: "A 404 error indicates that the webpage you're trying to reach can't be found. You might see a 404 error because of a problem with the website, because the page was moved or deleted, or because you typed the URL wrong."

3rd Party Cookie

According to Cookie-Script.com: "Third-party cookies are cookies that are set by a website other than the one you are currently on. For example, you can have a "Like" button on your website which will store a cookie on a visitor's computer, that cookie can later be accessed by Facebook to identify visitors and see which websites he visited. Such a cookie is considered to be a 3rd party cookie.". *Also see 'Cookie'.*

A/B-Testing

According to Optimizely: "A/B testing (also known as split testing or bucket testing) is a method of comparing two versions of a webpage or app against each other to determine which one performs better. AB testing is essentially an experiment where two or more variants of a page are shown to users at random, and statistical analysis is used to determine which variation performs better for a given conversion goal."

Above the Fold

According to Optimizely: "In the early days of publishing, 'above the fold' was a term used for content that appeared on the top half of the front page of a newspaper. When newspapers were displayed on a newsstand, the headlines and lead stories that appeared above the fold were the most visible, and catchy headlines and vivid imagery were commonly used to attract readers' attention, convincing them to buy the paper. As publishers moved their businesses online and web design evolved in the 1990's, the term continued to stick. Today, the fold no longer refers to an actual fold in a newspaper, but the bottom of a browser window, or approximately 600 pixels from the top of the page."

Account Based Marketing (ABM)

According to Hubspot: "A focused growth strategy in which Marketing and Sales collaborate to create personalized buying experiences for a mutually-identified set of high-value accounts."

Account Executive

According to Wikipedia: "Account executive is a role in advertising, marketing, and finance involving intimate understanding of a client company's objectives and products and a professional capability to provide effective advice toward creation of successful promotional activities and strategies.[1] The account executive directly works with, and provides services to, one or more delegate officers or executives of the client company. In IT organizations, an account executive is a senior management role, responsible for executing large contracts."

Account Portal

Defined by Diederik Martens as a landing page that is tailored and branded for a specific target account to discover new contacts in a company's decision making unit. *Also see 'prospect portal'.*

Active

A lead scoring dimension. It's the opposite of 'Latent'. It refers to pro-active behavior that can be seen as buying propensity signals (e.g., a person that fills out an event registration form).

Advertising

According to Wikipedia: "A marketing communication that employs an openly sponsored, non-personal message to promote or sell a product, service or idea."

Affiliate Marketing

According to "Shopify: "Affiliate marketing is an online sales tactic that lets a product owner increase sales by allowing others targeting the same audience—"affiliates"—to earn a commission by recommending the product to others. At the same time, it makes it possible for affiliates to earn money on product sales without creating products of their own. Simply put, affiliate marketing involves referring a product or service by sharing it on a blog, social media platforms, or website. The affiliate earns a commission each time someone makes a purchase through the unique link associated with their recommendation."

Agency

An advertising agency, marketing agency, digital agency, consulting agency, or software development firm that help their clients in business.

Agile

According to Wikipedia: "In software development, agile practices involve discovering requirements and developing solutions through the collaborative effort of self-organizing and cross-functional teams and their customers and/or end users. Agile learning generally refers to the transfer of agile methods of project work, especially Scrum, to learning processes. Likewise, Agile Learning proceeds in incremental steps and through an Iterative design which alternates between phases of learning and doing."

Ambassador

According to Wikipedia: "Predominantly, a brand ambassador is known as a positive spokesperson, an opinion leader or a community influencer, appointed as an internal or external agent to boost product or service sales and create brand awareness."

Alexa

According to Wikipedia: "According to Wikipedia: "Amazon Alexa, also known simply as Alexa, is a virtual assistant AI technology developed by Amazon, first used in the Amazon Echo smart speaker."

Alt-Text

According to MOZ: "Alt text (alternative text), also known as "alt attributes", "alt descriptions", or technically incorrectly as "alt tags," are used within an HTML code to describe the appearance and function of an image on a page. Using alt text on your images can make for a better user experience, but it may also help earn you both explicit and implicit SEO benefits. Along with implementing image title and file naming best practices, including alt text may also contribute to image SEO."". Also see 'Search Engine Optimization'.

Anchor

An anchor tag <a> is a HTML element that creates a hyperlink to a URL. The tag can wrap around text, images, or as buttons. It's a best practice to provide context about the destination of the hyperlink, by providing a clear anchor text (visible text) or by using the title attribute.

Appending

Data appending, according to NAICS, is a process that involves adding new data elements to an existing database. An example of a common data append would be the enhancement of a company's customer files. Companies often collect basic information on their clients such as phone numbers, emails, or addresses. A data append takes the information they have, matches it against a larger database of business data, allowing the desired missing data fields to be added.

Application Programming Interface (API)

According to Mulesoft: "API is the acronym for Application Programming Interface, which is a software intermediary that allows two applications to talk to each other. You may be familiar with the process of searching flights online. You have a variety of options to choose from, including different cities, departure and return dates, and more. Let us imagine that you're booking you are flight on an airline website. You choose a departure city and date, a return city and date, cabin class, as well as other variables. In order to book your flight, you interact with the airline's website to access their database and see if any seats are available on those dates and what the costs might be."

Artificial Intelligence (AI)

According to Wikipedia: "Artificial intelligence is intelligence demonstrated by machines, unlike the natural intelligence displayed by humans and animals."

Attribution

According to Chron.com: "Revenue attribution is the process of aligning or matching specific marketing costs to the sales revenue your company receives. Revenue attribution thus provides significant insights into what marketing campaigns and initiatives did or did not work and to what degree. It helps businesses better allocate marketing dollars and human resources to the marketing that customers respond to, thus saving your company time and money."

Attrition Rate

See 'Churn Rate'.

Awareness
The first of three phases in a simplified way of looking at the (B2B) buying process. The phase where you make potential buyers aware they might have a challenge that could require your products or services to solve it.

Backlink
According to MOZ: "A backlink is a link created when one website links to another. Backlinks are also called "inbound links" or "incoming links." Backlinks are important to SEO."

Backlog
According to Scrum.org: "The Sprint Backlog is a plan by and for the Developers. It is a highly visible, real-time picture of the work that the Developers plan to accomplish during the Sprint in order to achieve the Sprint Goal. Consequently, the Sprint Backlog is updated throughout the Sprint as more is learned. It should have enough detail that they can inspect their progress in the Daily Scrum."

Banner
According to MarketBusinessNews: "Banner ads are advertisements that companies and other organizations display on web pages. Typically, they consist of an image, video, or multimedia object. These types of ads may be still (static) or animated. The aim of the advertiser is to attract visitors to a specific website or remind consumers of a product, service, company, or brand."

BANT
According to MasterClass.com: "Created by IBM in the 1950s, BANT is a sales qualification methodology that helps salespeople identify qualified leads by focusing on four considerations: budget, authority, need, and timing. For sales teams, the main goal of BANT is to save time and shorten their sales cycles. A sales rep can use the BANT lead qualification process to weed out inadequate prospects and instead focus on leads who have a high probability of making a purchase."

Batch
According to Marketo: "A batch campaign launches at a specific time and affects a specific set of people all at once. An example would be sending an email to all people in California.". Also see 'Trigger'.

Bay Area

According to Wikipedia: "The Bay Area or simply the Bay, is a populous region surrounding the San Francisco, San Pablo, and Suisun Bay estuaries in Northern California. Economically, the post-war Bay Area saw huge growth in the financial and technology industries, creating a vibrant and diverse economy with a gross domestic product of over $700 billion, and home to the third highest concentration of Fortune 500 companies in the United States (as of 2018).". The Bay Area is well known for Sillicon Valley *(see 'Sillicon Valley').*

Best Practice

According to Wikipedia: "A best practice is a method or technique that has been generally accepted as superior to any alternatives because it produces results that are superior to those achieved by other means."

Big Hairy Audacious Goal (BHAG)

BHAG is a concept developed in the book Built to Last by Jim Collins. A BHAG (pronounced "Bee Hag," short for "Big Hairy Audacious Goal") is a powerful way to stimulate progress. A BHAG is clear and compelling, needing little explanation; people get it right away.

Bing

According to Lifewire: "Bing, sometimes also referred to as Bing Search, is a search engine developed by Microsoft and primarily known for being a search engine website accessible by visiting Bing.com.". Also see 'Google'.

Black Friday

According to BusinessInsider: "Most people know Black Friday as the day after Thanksgiving, when stores open early and offer various sales. These stores are often "in the black" (profitable) that day.". *Also see 'Cyber Monday'.*

Blog
According to Wikipedia: "A blog (a truncation of "weblog") is a discussion or informational website published on the World Wide Web consisting of discrete, often informal diary-style text entries (posts). Posts are typically displayed in reverse chronological order, so that the most recent post appears first, at the top of the web page. Until 2009, blogs were usually the work of a single individual, occasionally of a small group, and often covered a single subject or topic. In the 2010s, "multi-author blogs" (MABs) emerged, featuring the writing of multiple authors, and sometimes professionally edited. MABs from newspapers, other media outlets, universities, think tanks, advocacy groups, and similar institutions account for an increasing quantity of blog traffic."

Bottom-of-Funnel (BOFU)
See 'Top-of-Funnel'.

Bottleneck
A bottleneck is a critical point in a process. It is what stops or slows down a process and therefore requires extra attention.

Bounce
According to Wikipedia: "Bounce rate is a measure of "stickiness." The thinking being that an effective website will engage visitors deeper into the website. Encouraging visitors to continue with their visit. It is expressed as a percentage and represents the proportion of single page visits to total visits."

Brand
See 'Branding'.

Brand Awareness
According to Investopedia: "Brand awareness is a marketing term that describes the degree of consumer recognition of a product by its name. Creating brand awareness is a key step in promoting a new product or reviving an older brand. Ideally, awareness of the brand may include the qualities that distinguish the product from its competition.". Also see 'Branding'. *Also see 'Branding'.*

Branding

According to Entrepreneur.com: "An effective brand strategy gives you a major edge in increasingly competitive markets. But what exactly does "branding" mean? Simply put, your brand is your promise to your customer. It tells them what they can expect from your products and services, and it differentiates your offering from that of your competitors. Your brand is derived from who you are, who you want to be and who people perceive you to be. The foundation of your brand is your logo. Your website, packaging, and promotional materials--all of which should integrate your logo--communicate your brand. Your brand strategy is how, what, where, when and to whom you plan on communicating and delivering on your brand messages."

Brick & Mortar

According to Wikipedia: "Brick and mortar (also bricks and mortar or B&M) refers to a physical presence of an organization or business in a building or other structure. The term brick-and-mortar business is often used to refer to a company that possesses or leases retail shops, factory production facilities, or warehouses for its operations."

Business Intelligence (BI)

According to Tableau: "Business intelligence combines business analytics, data mining, data visualization, data tools and infrastructure, and best practices to help organizations to make more data-driven decisions."

Business-to-Business (B2B)

A business model where companies sell their products and services to other companies.

Business-to-Business-to-Consumer (B2B2C)

A business model where businesses reach new markets and customers (online) by partnering with consumer-oriented businesses.

Business-to-Consumer (B2C)

A business model where companies sell their products and services to consumers.

Business-to-Everyone (B2E)
According to Marketo: "The 'Creating Epic Customer Experiences' report shows how the B2B buying experience is more similar to B2C, giving rise to a "Business to Everyone," or "B2E" world. With 70% of B2B marketers saying they can't differentiate, B2E poses a new challenge for all business in an already competitive environment."

Business Unit
In a business unit structure, every business unit has its own profit and loss responsibility.

Buying Propensity
The likeliness that someone would buy your products or services.

Buying Stage
A phase in a simplified way of looking at the (B2B) buying process. E.g., Awareness, Consideration, and Decision.

Campaign
According to Investopedia: "Marketing campaigns promote products through different types of media, such as television, radio, print, and online platforms. Campaigns are not solely reliant on advertising and can include demonstrations, video conferencing, and other interactive techniques. Businesses operating in highly competitive markets and franchisees may initiate frequent marketing campaigns and devote significant resources to generating brand awareness and sales.". In Marketo Engage, a campaign can also refer to a workflow.

Canonical
According to Google: "A canonical URL is the URL of the page that Google thinks is most representative from a set of duplicate pages on your site. For example, if you have URLs for the same page

(for example: example.com?dress=1234 and example.com/dresses/1234),

Google chooses one as canonical. Note that the pages do not need to be absolutely identical; minor changes in sorting or filtering of list pages do not make the page unique (for example, sorting by price or filtering by item color)."

Case Study
According to MarTechAdvisor: "In marketing, a case study refers to any content that describes how your product or service has helped past customers in an attempt to convert leads into customers. Case studies are relevant for marketing B2B products, as you can gather data over time and outline how your product made a difference."

Cart Abandonment
According to Optimizely: "Shopping cart abandonment is when a potential customer starts a check out process for an online order but drops out of the process before completing the purchase. Any item that enters the shopping cart but never makes it through the transaction is considered to be "abandoned" by the shopper. Shopping cart abandonment is an important aspect of the online shopping process that retailers pay careful attention to."

CASL
According to Mailchimp: "The Canadian Anti-Spam Law (CASL) went into effect July 1, 2014. If you're in Canada or send a Commercial Electronic Message (CEM) to Canadian residents, you need to comply with CASL."

Change Management
According to Prosci: "Change management is the application of a structured process and set of tools for leading the people side of change to achieve a desired outcome. Ultimately, change management focuses on how to help people engage, adopt and use a change in their day-to-day work."

Chaploop™
The Chaploop™ methodology enables you to consistently grow your business through MarTech. Your company's marketing technology stack is like a 'growthhackers' toolbox to test new marketing and sales ideas, for business boosting hypotheses, and then scale those ideas that work.

Churn Rate

According to Wikipedia: "Churn rate (sometimes called attrition rate), when applied to a customer base, refers to the proportion of contractual customers or subscribers who leave a supplier during a given time period. It is a possible indicator of customer dissatisfaction, cheaper and/or better offers from the competition, more successful sales and/or marketing by the competition, or reasons having to do with the customer life cycle.". *Also see 'Customer Retention'.*

Cleansing

According to Tableau: "Data cleaning is the process of fixing or removing incorrect, corrupted, incorrectly formatted, duplicate, or incomplete data within a dataset. When combining multiple data sources, there are many opportunities for data to be duplicated or mislabeled. If data is incorrect, outcomes and algorithms are unreliable, even though they may look correct."

C-Level (e.g., CMO, CRO, CPO, CEO, CIO, CTO, CDO, or COO)

According to Investopedia: "C-suite, or C-level, is widely-used vernacular describing a cluster of a corporation's most important senior executives. C-suite gets its name from the titles of top senior executives, which tend to start with the letter C, for "chief," as in chief executive officer (CEO), chief financial officer (CFO), chief operating officer (COO), and chief information officer (CIO). C-level members work together to ensure a company stays true to its established plans and policies."

Click-Through-Rate (CTR)

According to Wikipedia: "Click-through rate (CTR) is the ratio of users who click on a specific link to the number of total users who view a page, email, or advertisement. It is commonly used to measure the success of an online advertising campaign for a particular website as well as the effectiveness of email campaigns."

Closed-Loop

According to Hubspot: "Closed-loop marketing is marketing that relies on data and insights from closed-loop reporting. "Closing the loop" just means that sales teams report to Marketing about what happened to the leads that they received, which helps Marketing understand their best and worst lead sources."

Cohort Analysis

According to Clevertap: "Cohort analysis is a subset of behavioral analytics that takes the data from a given eCommerce platform, web application, or online game and rather than looking at all users as one unit, it breaks them into related groups for analysis. These related groups, or cohorts, usually share common characteristics or experiences within a defined time-span. Cohort analysis is a tool to measure user engagement over time. It helps to know whether user engagement is actually getting better over time or is only appearing to improve because of growth."

Comma Separated Value (CSV)

According to Wikipedia: "A delimited text file that uses a comma to separate values. Each line of the file is a data record. Each record consists of one or more fields, separated by commas.". Often used to export and import data between different technology platforms to exchange data.

Complex Sale

"Mastering the Complex Sale" is a book by strategist Jeff Thull. Selling is more challenging in this era of complexity. Selling means managing decisions, changes, expectations, and relationships. He defines several traps to avoid, like the assumption trap, presentation trap, and adversarial trap.

Consideration

The second of three phases in a simplified way of looking at the (B2B) buying process. The phase where potential buyers educate themselves on how to solve their challenges.

Consumer

According to Wikipedia: "A consumer is a person or a group who intends to order, orders, or uses purchased goods, products, or services primarily for personal, social, family, household and similar needs, not directly related to entrepreneurial or business activities."

Content

See 'Content Marketing'.

Content Management System (CMS)

According to Wikipedia: "A content management system is a computer software used to manage the creation and modification of digital content. CMSs are typically used for enterprise content management (ECM) and web content management (WCM).". According to Optimizely: "A content management system (CMS) is an application that is used to manage web content, allowing multiple contributors to create, edit and publish. Content in a CMS is typically stored in a database and displayed in a presentation layer based on a set of templates."

Content Marketing

According to Content Marketing Institute: "Content marketing is a strategic marketing approach focused on creating and distributing valuable, relevant, and consistent content to attract and retain a clearly defined audience — and, ultimately, to drive profitable customer action."

Content Marketing Matrix (by Smart Insights)

According to Smart Insights: "A content marketing planning tool to help marketers generate ideas for the most engaging content types for their audiences."

Content Marketing Pyramid™

According to Curata: "A strategic framework enabling you to execute a content campaign, assuring optimal content consumption, reuse, and reach. A strategy for generating more with less."

Conversion

According to Optimizely: "The conversion rate is the number of conversions divided by the total number of visitors. For example, if an ecommerce site receives 200 visitors in a month and has 50 sales, the conversion rate would be 50 divided by 200, or 25%."

Conversational Marketing

According to Drift, who coined the term 'conversational marketing,' it is: "The fastest way to move buyers through your marketing and sales funnels through the power of real-time conversations. It builds relationships and creates authentic experiences with customers and buyers."

Cookie

According to ChooseToEncrypt: "Cookies are small files stored in your browser that help websites you visit often identify you. Websites use cookies to store your custom settings and preferences or log-in information."

Copywriting

According to Wikipedia: "Copywriting is the act or occupation of writing text for the purpose of advertising or other forms of marketing. The product, called copy or sales copy, is written content that aims to increase brand awareness and ultimately persuade a person or group to take a particular action."

Cost Per Acquisition (CPA)

See 'Customer Acquisition Cost (CAC)'.

Cost Per Lead (CPL)

See 'Customer Acquisition Cost (CAC)'.

Crawl

According to Wikipedia: "A Web crawler, sometimes called a spider or spiderbot and often shortened to crawler, is an Internet bot that systematically browses the World Wide Web, typically operated by search engines for the purpose of Web indexing."

Cross-Selling

According to Shopify: "It's easy to confuse cross-selling with upselling. Cross-selling involves offering the customer a related product or service, while upselling typically involves trading up to a better version of what's being purchased.".

Crowdsourcing

According to Business2Community: "Since the 2004 publication of James Surowiecki's highly influential book, The Wisdom of Crowds, the idea that large groups of people can be smarter than a few individuals, no matter how brilliant, has been gradually gaining prominence in academic circles, business communities, and public opinion. Crowdsourcing is one of the most popular applications of this idea. Numerous organizations –including corporations, governmental agencies, and non-profits – have adopted crowdsourcing as an innovation tool to help them address their most pressing business challenges. However, the practical adoption of crowdsourcing has been far from seamless. Why? Firstly, there is widespread, often completely paralyzing, uncertainty over which business challenges can (or can't) be solved by crowdsourcing. Secondly, many organizations – especially those new to crowdsourcing – have difficulty "matching" their specific problems to the crowdsourcing platform which is most suitable for solving them."

Customer Acquisition

According to DemandJump: "Customer acquisition refers to bringing in new customers - or convincing people to buy your products. It is a process used to bring consumers down the marketing funnel from brand awareness to purchase decision.". *Also see 'Customer Acquisition Cost'.*

Customer Acquisition Cost (CAC)

According to Lead-Case.com: "CAC specifically measures the cost of acquiring an actually paying user (a customer). On the other hand, CPA (cost per acquisition) measures the cost of acquiring a non-paying user (not a customer), for example, cost per lead (CPL), cost per signup, cost per registration or cost per activation. Let's review some examples.".

Customer Data Platform (CDP)

According to Wikipedia: "A customer data platform is a collection of software which creates a persistent, unified customer database that is accessible to other systems. Data is pulled from multiple sources, cleaned and combined to create a single customer profile."

Customer Insights

According to TrustPilot: "A consumer insight is an interpretation used by businesses to gain a deeper understanding of how their audience thinks and feels. Analyzing human behaviors allows companies to really understand what their consumers want and need, and most importantly, why they feel this way. When consumer insight research is conducted properly, it should improve the effectiveness of how a company communicates to its customers, which is likely to change consumer behavior, and therefore increase sales."

Customer Lifetime Value (CLV)

According to Qualtrics: "Customer lifetime value is the total worth to a business of a customer over the whole period of their relationship. It's an important metric as it costs less to keep existing customers than it does to acquire new ones, so increasing the value of your existing customers is a great way to drive growth. Knowing the CLV helps businesses develop strategies to acquire new customers and retain existing ones while maintaining profit margins."

Customer Loyalty

According to Hubspot: "Customer loyalty is a customer's willingness to repeatedly return to a company to conduct business. This is typically due to the delightful and remarkable experiences they have with that brand."

Customer Relations Management (CRM)

According to Wikipedia: "CRM systems compile data from a range of different communication channels, including a company's website, telephone, email, live chat, marketing materials and more recently, social media. They allow businesses to learn more about their target audiences and how to best cater for their needs, thus retaining customers and driving sales growth. CRM may be used with past, present or potential customers."

Customer Retention
According to Wikipedia: "Customer retention refers to the ability of a company or product to retain its customers over some specified period. High customer retention means customers of the product or business tend to return to, continue to buy or in some other way not defect to another product or business, or to non-use entirely.". *Also see 'Churn Rate'.*

Customer Satisfaction (CSAT)
According to Survicate: "Defined as a measurement that determines how products or services provided by a company meet customer expectations. Customer satisfaction is one of the most important indicators of consumer purchase intentions and loyalty.". CSAT is often expressed as a score from 1 to 10, where 10 reflects the highest rate of satisfaction. *Also see 'Net promotor Score (NPS)'.*

Customer Service
According to Salesforce: "Customer service is the support you offer your customers — both before and after they buy and use your products or services — that helps them have an easy and enjoyable experience with you. Offering amazing customer service is important if you want to retain customers and grow your business."

Customer Story
Where a case study describes how a product or service has helped a particular client in a specific scenario and/or project, a customer story overarches the larger (transformation) journey a client has, spanning multiple projects and case studies.

Cyber Monday
According to Wikipedia: "Cyber Monday is a marketing term for e-commerce transactions on the Monday after Thanksgiving in the United States. It was created by retailers to encourage people to shop online.". Also see 'Black Friday'.

Dashboard
According to Klipfolio: "A data dashboard is an information management tool that visually tracks, analyzes, and displays key performance indicators (KPI), metrics and key data points to monitor the health of a business, department or specific process."

Data Driven Decision Making (DDDM)

According to Harvard Business School: "Data-driven decision-making is the process of using data to inform your decision-making process and validate a course of action before committing to it."

Data Management Platform (DMP)

According to Wikipedia: "A data management platform is a software platform used for collecting and managing data. They allow businesses to identify audience segments, which can be used to target specific users and contexts in online advertising campaigns. DMPs may use big data and artificial intelligence algorithms to process and analyze large data sets about users from various sources."

Data Quality

According to Wikipedia: "Data quality refers to the state of qualitative or quantitative pieces of information. There are many definitions of data quality, but data is generally considered high quality if it is "fit for [its] intended uses in operations, decision making and planning"."

Database

A database is a collection of organized data, generally stored and accessed electronically from a computer system. A marketing database stores data on customer properties as well as data on their interactions. Also *see 'CRM'*.

Deal

According to Cambridge Dictionary: "An agreement or an arrangement, especially in business."

Decision

The third of three phases in a simplified way of looking at the (B2B) buying process. The phase where potential buyers know how they want to solve their challenges, but are now evaluating who they're going to buy the solution from.

Decision Making Unit (DMU)

According to Oxford Reference: "Individuals and groups participating in a buying decision in an industrial purchasing process. They share some common goals and are knowledgeable about the risks arising from decisions. Members of the group may be initiators, influencers, deciders, approvers, gatekeepers, buyers, or users. See buyer and buying behavior."

Demand
See 'Demand Generation'.

Demand Generation
According to Drift: "Demand generation refers to any activity that drives awareness and interest in your product or service with the ultimate goal to create a predictable pipeline that will grow your business. It's an umbrella term that covers all your marketing and sales initiatives from every touchpoint in the customer's journey—from initial prospect interest to upselling customers."

Demand Waterfall™
The SiriusDecisions Demand Waterfall® is a shared view between marketing and sales of a B2B organization's ability to generate new business. *Also see 'SiriusDecisions'.*

Demographics
According to Wikipedia: "Demographic profiling is a form of demographic analysis used by marketers so that they may be as efficient as possible with advertising products or services and identifying any possible gaps in their marketing strategy."

Development
According to Wikipedia: "Software development is the process of conceiving, specifying, designing, programming, documenting, testing, and bug fixing involved in creating and maintaining applications, frameworks, or other software components."

Digital Marketing
According to Marketo: "Engagement marketing is the method of forming meaningful interactions with potential and returning customers based on the data you collect over time. By engaging customers in a digital landscape, you build brand awareness, set yourself as an industry thought leader, and place your business at the forefront when the customer is ready to buy."

Digital Marketing Maturity Growth Model
A model by Diederik Martens to uncover growth potential in digital marketing in different categories.

Disqualifying

According to InsightSquared: "Badly-qualified prospects lead to two significant issues within your company, both of which lose you revenue. By using up valuable sales reps on leads that are going nowhere, you are both wasting their time (and your money), and inflating your pipeline with dead end prospects.". *Also see 'Rejecting' and 'Recycling'.*

Eloqua

Oracle CX, previously Oracle Marketing Cloud, previously Eloqua, is a marketing automation platform. *See "Marketing Automation".*

End-to-End Conversion

See 'Closed-Loop'.

Engagement

According to Marketo: "Engagement marketing is the use of strategic, resourceful content to engage people and create meaningful interactions over time."

Epic

According to Atlassian: "An epic is a large body of work that can be broken down into a number of smaller stories. Epics often encompass multiple teams, on multiple projects. Epics are almost always delivered over a set of sprints."

Event Driven Marketing

A significant event can be a major happening in a customer's life. They can lead to a measurable change in a customer's normal behavior, state of mind, personal circumstance, or interaction pattern. It offers a reason to communicate with the customer, with a relevant proposal, at the right time.

Explicit

A lead scoring dimension. It's the opposite of 'Implicit'. It refers data that is directly provided by the prospect or customer. Which can then be used for the purpose of scoring buying propensity (e.g., A person fills out his/her job title in a form.).

Firmographics

According to Wikipedia: "What demographics are to people, firmographics are to organizations. However, Webster (2005) suggested that the term "firmographics" is a combination of demographics and geographics."

Form

According to Wikipedia: "A webform, web form or HTML form on a web page allows a user to enter data that is sent to a server for processing. Forms can resemble paper or database forms because web users fill out the forms using checkboxes, radio buttons, or text fields. For example, forms can be used to enter shipping or credit card data to order a product, or can be used to retrieve search results from a search engine."

Gated Content

Content that is only made available after a person fills out a form. Opposite of 'Ungated Content'. *Also see 'Content' and 'Form'.*

Google Adwords

According to Wikipedia: "Google Ads, formerly Google AdWords, is an online advertising platform developed by Google, where advertisers bid to display brief advertisements, service offerings, product listings, or videos to web users. It can place ads both in the results of search engines like Google Search (the Google Search Network) and on non-search websites, mobile apps, and videos (the Google Display Network). Services are offered under a pay-per-click (PPC) pricing model.". *Also see 'Pay-per-Click'.*

Google Analytics

According to Wikipedia: "A web analytics service offered by Google that tracks and reports website traffic, currently as a platform inside the Google Marketing Platform brand."

Growth Hacking
According to Wikipedia: "Growth Hacking is a relatively new focus within the field of marketing focused on the growth of a company. It is both referred to as a process as a set of cross-disciplinary (digital) skills. The goal is to rapidly test ideas that can improve the customer journey, and replicate and scale the ideas that work and modify or abandon the ones that don't before investing a lot of resources. It started in relation to early-stage start-ups who need rapid growth within short time on tight budgets, and also reached bigger corporate companies."

HubSpot
Hubspot is an inbound marketing platform, which offers marketing automation functionalities. *See "Marketing Automation".*

Humanistic Marketing
Companies need to develop more empathy. Customers want to be seen and heard. Having a personalized experience is far more effective to create a memorable and positive experience. Shift from servicing to really helping customers in their lives.

Implicit
A lead scoring dimension. It's the opposite of 'Explicit'. It refers data that is indirectly interpreted for the prospect or customer. Which can then be used for the purpose of scoring buying propensity (e.g., A person visits a webpage of a job vacancy, which suggests he/she might be more interested in working at the company, rather than buying a product from it.).

Inferred Data
Data that is automatically generated for a person in CRM and/or marketing automation. Typically through Reverse IP-Lookup. E.g., country, based in IP-address or company name, based on email address.

Influencer

According to WIRED: "Influencer culture, as we know it today, is inextricably tied to consumerism and the rise of technology. The term is shorthand for someone (or something) with the power to affect the buying habits or quantifiable actions of others by uploading some form of original—often sponsored—content to social media platforms like Instagram, YouTube, Snapchat, or God forbid, LinkedIn. Be it moody photos, cheeky video reviews, meandering blogs, or blurry soon-to-disappear Stories, the value of the content in question is derived from the perceived authority—and, most importantly, authenticity—of its creator."

Inquiry

An inquiry, often also called 'Handraise', is when a potential buyer indicates intend and/or reaches out to a company. On many occasions there is overlap with an anonymous visitor becoming know (to the system). Typically by filling out a web form.

Integration

According to Wikipedia: "Data integration involves combining data residing in different sources and providing users with a unified view of them. This process becomes significant in a variety of situations, which include both commercial (such as when two similar companies need to merge their databases).". E.g., integrating CRM and marketing automation.

Intend

Intend Data, according to Bombora, is: "Data that is collected about business web users' observed behavior -specifically web content consumption- that provides insights into their interests and from this indicate potential intent to take an action."

IP-Address

According to Kaspersky: "An IP-address is a unique address that identifies a device on the internet or a local network. IP stands for "Internet Protocol," which is the set of rules governing the format of data sent via the internet or local network."

IP-Lookup

According to WhatsMyIP.com: "An IP-address lookup will determine the location of any IP address. The results have quite a bit of information. The results include information like the city, state/region, postal/zip code, country name, ISP, and time zone."

JavaScript

See 'Script'.

Journey

According to Hubspot: "The buyer's journey describes a buyer's path to purchase. In other words, buyers don't wake up and decide to buy on a whim. They go through a process to become aware of, consider and evaluate, and decide to purchase a new product or service."

jQuery

See 'Script'.

Keynote

According to Wikipedia: "A keynote in public speaking is a talk that establishes a main underlying theme. In corporate or commercial settings, greater importance is attached to the delivery of a keynote speech or keynote address. The keynote establishes the framework for the following programs of events or convention agenda. Increasingly the word keynote is being used as a synonym for plenary session or "invited talk," with some conferences having an opening keynote, a closing keynote, and many other keynotes."

Landing Page

According to Unbounce: "In digital marketing, a landing page is a standalone web page, created specifically for a marketing or advertising campaign. It's where a visitor "lands" after they click on a link in an email, or ads from Google, Bing, YouTube, Facebook, Instagram, Twitter, or similar places on the web. Unlike web pages, which typically have many goals and encourage exploration, landing pages are designed with a single focus or goal, known as a call to action (or CTA, for short)."

Latent

A lead scoring dimension. It's the opposite of 'Active'. It refers to re-active behavior for the purpose of scoring buying propensity (e.g., a person that opens an email that you have sent).

Lead

According to Wikipedia: "In marketing, lead generation is the initiation of consumer interest or enquiry into products or services of a business. Leads can be created for purposes such as list building, e-newsletter list acquisition or for sales leads. Lead generation is often paired with lead management to move leads through the purchase funnel. This combination of activities is referred to as pipeline marketing."

Lead Generation

See 'Demand Generation'.

Lead Management

According to Wikipedia: "Lead management is a set of methodologies, systems, and practices designed to generate new potential business clientele, generally operated through a variety of marketing campaigns or programs."

Lifecycle

According to CampaignMonitor: "In general, the customer lifecycle in marketing refers to the beginning of the customer experience through to the end, which is typically a purchase. A customer journey, however, varies in that the cycle doesn't stop. Instead, the consumer moves through additional stages that help them become familiar with your services or products, come back for more, and even helps you by spreading the word of your brand to others around them."

LinkedIn

Owned by Microsoft. According to BusinessInsider: "LinkedIn is a professional networking site, designed to help people make business connections, share their experiences and resumes, and find jobs."

Longlist

see 'Shortlist'.

Machine Learning

According to SAS: "Machine learning is a method of data analysis that automates analytical model building. It is a branch of artificial intelligence based on the idea that systems can learn from data, identify patterns and make decisions with minimal human intervention."

MailChimp
An email automation platform.

Marketer / Marketeer
According to Oxford Dictionary: "Person who sells goods or services in a market."

Marketing
According to AMA.org: "Marketing is the activity, set of institutions, and processes for creating, communicating, delivering, and exchanging offerings that have value for customers, clients, partners, and society at large."

Marketing Automation Platform (MAP)
See 'Marketing Automation'.

Marketing Automation
According to Diederik Martens: ""A practice by marketers to plan, manage, coordinate, test, improve and measure their marketing efforts, both online and offline, through technology, processes, data, and best practices. To also streamline marketing and sales and closely manage and nurture generated leads, aiming to convert leads into customers. To also upsell, cross sell, and retain customers. And to inform, engage, and satisfy customers and create brand ambassadors.""

Marketing Intelligence
See 'Business Intelligence'.

Marketing Maturity
Gartner assesses an organization's marketing maturity against nine different competencies: Innovation, Operations, Marketing Analytics, Digital Commerce, Mobile, Social, Multichannel Marketing, Customer Experience, and Resources.

Marketing Operations (MOps)
Loosely based on SiriusDecisions definition, Diederik defines marketing operations as: "Marketing Operations (MOps) plays a crucial role in aligning strategy and processes throughout the organization to ensure that they are able to excel in their marketing efforts. Whether leveraging technology, creating processes, productizing best-practices, coordinating functions, training, reporting on performance, or generating new insights, a Marketing Operations is at the center of much of the marketing organization's activities."

Marketo
Marketo Engage, part of the Adobe Experience Cloud, is an engagement platform, which offers (predominantly B2B) marketing automation functionalities. *See "Marketing Automation".*

MarTech
According to Bynder: "Marketing technology, or MarTech, helps to make the life of any marketer much easier. Marketing technology is a general term for tech used to assist marketing teams in their work. The technology is mostly used in the sphere of digital marketing, and also for the optimization of offline marketing channels."

MarTech Landscape
The marketing technology sector has grown substantially since it was first identified as a standalone industry in 2011. At that time, the number of major vendors of Martech Landscape by Scott Brinker stood at around 150; in 2018 this figure has grown to approximately 7000.

Marketing Qualified Lead (MQL)
According to Tableau: "A Marketing Qualified Lead is a lead who has indicated interest in what a brand has to offer based on marketing efforts or is otherwise more likely to become a customer than other leads."

Middle-of-Funnel (MOFU)
See 'Top-of-Funnel'.

Minimum Viable Product (MVP)
According to Wikipedia: "A minimum viable product is a version of a (software) product with just enough features to be usable by early customers who can then provide feedback for future product development."

Multi-Channel
According to Shopify: "Multichannel blends the customer experience and gives consumers choice to engage on the channel they prefer. It's flexible but expects brands to behave in the confines of the channel.". *Also see 'Omni-Channel.'*

Munchkin
Tracking script from Marketo Engage. *See 'Tracking'.*

MySQL
According to Wikipedia: "MySQL is an open-source relational database management system (RDBMS). A relational database organizes data into one or more data tables in which data types may be related to each other; these relations help structure the data."

New Name
See 'Inquiry'.

Nurture Content Pyramid
A variation by Diederik Martens on the well-known 'Content Pyramid'.

Nurturing
According to Marketo: "Lead nurturing consists of cross-channel communication that combines content marketing and marketing automation to create a system that builds and maintains relationships with customers."

Omni-Channel
According to Bloomreach: "Omni-channel retail (or omnichannel commerce) is a multichannel approach to sales that focus on providing seamless customer experience whether the client is shopping online from a mobile device, a laptop or in a brick-and-mortar store.". *Also see 'Multi-Channel.'*

Opportunity
According to Salesforce: "In Salesforce, an opportunity is a sale or pending deal. Multiple opportunities make up your sales pipeline, which contributes to your sales forecast."

Pay-per-Click (PPC)
According to WordStream: "a model of internet marketing in which advertisers pay a fee each time one of their ads is clicked. Essentially, it's a way of buying visits to your site, rather than attempting to "earn" those visits organically.".

Persona
According to Buyer Persona Institute: "Built from the real words of real buyers, a buyer persona tells you what prospective customers are thinking and doing as they weigh their options to address a problem that your company resolves. Much more than a one-dimensional profile of the people you need to influence, or a map of their journey, actionable buyer personas reveal insights about your buyers' decisions -- the specific attitudes, concerns and criteria that drive prospective customers to choose you, your competitor or the status quo."

Pipeline
See 'Opportunity'.

Pitfall
When growing and innovating you should avoid common pitfalls. Also called hazards. Opposite of 'Best-Practice'. According to Wikipedia: "A hazard is a potential source of harm. Substances, events, or circumstances can constitute hazards when their nature would allow them, even just theoretically, to cause damage to health, life, property, or any other interest of value.". *Also see 'Best Practice'.*

Predictive

According to Wikipedia: "Predictive analytics encompasses a variety of statistical techniques from data mining, predictive modelling, and machine learning that analyze current and historical facts to make predictions about future or otherwise unknown events. In business, predictive models exploit patterns found in historical and transactional data to identify risks and opportunities. Models capture relationships among many factors to allow assessment of risk or potential associated with a particular set of conditions, guiding decision-making for candidate transactions."

Program

Marketo Engage jargon. A container for a marketing initiative that encompasses one or more workflows (campaigns) and assets (e.g., emails, landing pages).

Proof-of-Concept (PoC)

According to Wikipedia: "Proof of concept, also known as proof of principle, is a realization of a certain method or idea in order to demonstrate its feasibility, or a demonstration in principle with the aim of verifying that some concept or theory has practical potential. A proof of concept is usually small and may or may not be complete."

Proposal

According to Wikipedia: "A term of business proposal is a written offer from a seller to a prospective sponsor. Business proposals are often a key step in the complex sales process—i.e., whenever a buyer considers more than price in a purchase."

Proposition

According to Wikipedia: "A value proposition is a promise of value to be delivered, communicated, and acknowledged. It is also a belief from the customer about how value (benefit) will be delivered, experienced, and acquired. Creating a value proposition is a part of business strategy. Kaplan and Norton say 'Strategy is based on a differentiated customer value proposition. Satisfying customers is the source of sustainable value creation.'"

Prospect

According to TheBalanceSMB: "A prospect is a potential customer who has been qualified as fitting certain criteria outlined by a company based on its business offerings. Determining if a contact is a sales prospect is the first step in the selling process."

Prospect Portal

What Diederik Martens defines as a landing page to support closing the deal and that is tailored and branded for a specific prospect. Targeted the yet known and unknown contact in the company's decision making unit. *Also see 'Account Portal'.*

Quarterly Business Review (QBR)

According to GainSight: "Also known as a Business Review or an Executive Business Review, a QBR is, at its most basic, just a once-per-quarter meeting with your customer.". Though a company can also conduct an internal QBR with stakeholders from Sales, Marketing, Support, and other departments.

Query Parameter

A query string is a part of a uniform resource locator, also known as URL (e.g., https://diederikmartens.com), that assigns values to specified query_parameters (e.g., ?key=value).

Queue

Queues (in Salesforce) are like holding areas in your CRM, where leads wait for a marketing and/or sales user to pick up and assign them to an owner, after which they follow-up.

Recycling

Sales can either disqualify or reject an MQL. A disqualified lead is trashes, while a rejected lead can be recycled by marketing. When marketing thinks the lead is ready to be put in front of sales again, they'll mark it as MQL again. *Also see 'Rejecting' and 'Disqualifying'.*

Rejecting

See 'Recycling'.

Request-for-Information (RFI)

According to Wikipedia: "A request for information (RFI) is a common business process whose purpose is to collect written information about the capabilities of various suppliers."

Request-for-Proposal (RFP)

According to Wikipedia: "A request for proposal is a document that solicits proposal, often made through a bidding process, by an agency or company interested in procurement of a commodity, service, or valuable asset, to potential suppliers to submit business proposals. It is submitted early in the procurement cycle, either at the preliminary study, or procurement stage."

Retargeting

According to MailChimp: "Retargeting campaigns remind your website visitors of your products and services after they leave your website without buying."

Return-on-Investment (ROI)

According to Investopedia: "A performance measure used to evaluate the efficiency or profitability of an investment or compare the efficiency of a number of different investments. ROI tries to directly measure the amount of return on a particular investment, relative to the investment's cost. To calculate ROI, the benefit (or return) of an investment is divided by the cost of the investment. The result is expressed as a percentage or a ratio."

Sales

According to Wikipedia: "Sales are activities related to selling or the number of goods sold in a given targeted time period. The delivery of a service for a cost is also considered a sale."

Sales Accepted/Assigned Lead (SAL)

SiriusDecisions defines the sales accepted lead (SAL) stage of the demand creation process as a formal process for acceptance of leads by inside, field or channel sales. Salespeople who accept leads are simply acknowledging that the leads they've received meet the agreed-upon criteria in the SLA.

Sales Automation

According to LeadSquared: "Sales automation takes all these time-consuming tasks that are performed every day, week, or month, as well as other tasks that are triggered by a certain event and runs them for you. This makes everything (and everyone) more efficient and has a direct relationship with the revenue generated by the sales team."

Sales Enablement
According to NewBreedRevenue: "Sales enablement is a combination of coaching, tools and content to help your sales team be more efficient and effective. Your sales team needs to be properly enabled to carry out a successful sales strategy. By providing key elements of sales enablement, you allow your team to work better within an inbound sales process so that they can provide contextually relevant information, carry out helpful conversations and see — in real-time — which of their efforts are working."

Sales Operations (SOps)
According to SalesHacker: "Sales operations refers to the unit, role, activities, and processes within a sales organization that support, enable, and drive front line sales teams to sell better, faster, and more efficiently. Through strategically implemented training, software tools and engagement techniques, sales ops leaders enable sales reps to focus more on selling in order to drive business results."

Sales Qualified Lead (SQL)
According to NewBreedRevenue: "Typically, a meeting is involved for an MQL to become an SQL. That meeting can be a demo, an assessment or even just a discovery call, but a conversation between the prospect and a sales rep should occur at this stage. The contact only becomes an opportunity if during this conversation they confirm interest in continuing the sales process and potentially making a purchase. Of course, this procedure can look different for every single company.". Many companies have the policy that when an MQL (which should be contactable) is accepted (so SAL), they must reach out for that call or meeting. Thus for many companies an SAL is a lead that will be contacted at all times. In those cases an SQL is considered to be equal to when an opportunity is created after the call or meeting.

Salesforce (SFDC)
Salesforce.com provides customer relationship management (CRM) services and also provides a complementary suite of enterprise applications focused on customer service, sales automation, marketing automation, analytics, and application development.

Scalable Mindset
Having a mindset for developing growth. What works today, should also work on a larger scale tomorrow.

Scale-up

According to Wikipedia: "A scaleup can be identified as being in the "growth phase" life-cycle in the Millers and Friesen (1984) life cycle theorem, or the "Direction phase" in the Greiner growth curve.". *Also see 'Start-Up'.*

Scoring

Lead scoring in marketing automation is basically assigning points to properties and behavior that implies propensity to buy. Leads with higher scores should have a higher propensity to buy.

Script

For webpages often short for JavaScript by marketers. According to Wikipedia: "A scripting language or script language is a programming language for a runtime system that automates the execution of tasks that would otherwise be performed individually by a human operator."

Scrum

See 'Agile'

Search Engine Advertising (SEA)

According to Ryte: "Search-engine advertising (SEA) is a branch of online marketing. Advertisements in the form of a text or images are posted on search engines such as Google or Bing. These ads then appear prominently in the search engine results pages (SERP)."

Search Engine Marketing (SEM)

A category of marketing for search engines, like Google, that includes 'Search Engine Advertising' and 'Search Engine Optimization'.

Search Engine Optimization (SEO)

According to SearchEngineLand: "SEO stands for "search engine optimization." In simple terms, it means the process of improving your site to increase its visibility for relevant searches."

Shortlist

A shortlist, used in selection processes by buyers, is a list of suppliers that has been reduced from a longer list (longlist) of suppliers. Narrowing down. The buyer will most likely buy at one of the suppliers on the shortlist. *Also see 'Longlist'.*

Silicon Valley
According to Wikipedia: "Silicon Valley is a region in the southern part of the Bay Area in Northern California that serves as a global center for high technology and innovation. The word "silicon" in the name originally referred to the large number of innovators and manufacturers in the region specializing in silicon-based circuit chips. The area is now home to many of the world's largest high-tech corporations, including the headquarters of more than 30 businesses in the Fortune 1000, and thousands of start-up companies."

SiriusDecisions
According to Wikipedia: "SiriusDecisions, Inc. is a global B2B research and advisory firm with headquarters in Wilton, Connecticut. The company provides advisory, consulting and learning services to help executives improve the performance of their sales, marketing, and product strategies. SiriusDecisions developed the "Demand Waterfall" model, which is widely used by B2B companies to describe and measure their lead-to-revenue funnel."

Sitecore
A content management system (CMS) that provided multiple additional features. *See 'Content Management System'.*

Small Medium Business (SMB)
According to Wikipedia: "Small and medium-sized enterprises (SMEs) or small and medium-sized businesses (SMBs) are businesses whose personnel numbers fall below certain limits. According to the European Commission, MEs are enterprises which have less than 250 staff headcount and less than €50M turnover. SEs have less than 50 staff headcount and less than €10M turnover. The United States has a typical cap of 500 staffcount and less than $100M in annual sales. Both the US and the EU generally use the same threshold of fewer than 10 employees for small offices (SOHO).". According to Wikipedia: "Social media marketing is becoming more popular for both practitioners and researchers. Most social media platforms have built-in data analytics tools, enabling companies to track the progress, success, and engagement of ad campaigns."

Small Medium Enterprise (SME)
See 'SMB'.

Media

According to Wikipedia: "Social media are interactive technologies that allow the creation or sharing/exchange of information, ideas, career interests, and other forms of expression via virtual communities and networks.". Examples are LinkedIn, Twitter, Facebook, Instagram, and TikTok.

Social Media Sharing Model

Which bottlenecks need be addressed when using social media in marketing campaigns to increase the chance of going viral. A concept by Diederik Martens. *Also see 'Viral'.*

Small Office / Home Office (SOHO)

See 'SMB'.

Spaghetti Statistics

Slang for questionable statistical outcomes and/or statistical significance. According to Harvard Business Review, statistical significance is: "Statistical significance helps quantify whether a result is likely due to chance or to some factor of interest," says Redman. When a finding is significant, it simply means you can feel confident that's it real, not that you just got lucky (or unlucky) in choosing the sample.". *Also see 'Statistics'.*

Sprint

According to Scrum.org: "They are fixed length events of one month or less to create consistency. A new Sprint starts immediately after the conclusion of the previous Sprint. All the work necessary to achieve the Product Goal, including Sprint Planning, Daily Scrums, Sprint Review, and Sprint Retrospective, happen within Sprints. During the Sprint: No changes are made that would endanger the Sprint Goal; Quality does not decrease; The Product Backlog is refined as needed; and scope may be clarified and renegotiated with the Product Owner as more is learned. Sprints enable predictability by ensuring inspection and adaptation of progress toward a Product Goal at least every calendar month. When a Sprint's horizon is too long the Sprint Goal may become invalid, complexity may rise, and risk may increase. Shorter Sprints can be employed to generate more learning cycles and limit risk of cost and effort to a smaller time frame. Each Sprint may be considered a short project."

Stand-Up

According to Scrum.org: "The purpose of the Daily Scrum is to inspect progress toward the Sprint Goal and adapt the Sprint Backlog as necessary, adjusting the upcoming planned work. The Daily Scrum is a 15-minute event for the Developers of the Scrum Team. To reduce complexity, it is held at the same time and place every working day of the Sprint. The Developers can select whatever structure and techniques they want, as long as their Daily Scrum focuses on progress toward the Sprint Goal and produces an actionable plan for the next day of work. This creates focus and improves self-management. Daily Scrums improve communications, identify impediments, promote quick decision-making, and consequently eliminate the need for other meetings."

Start-Up

According to Wikipedia: "A start-up or start-up is a company or project undertaken by an entrepreneur to seek, develop, and validate a scalable economic model.". *Also see 'Scale-Up'.*

Statistics

According to Investopedia: "Statistics is the study and manipulation of data, including ways to gather, review, analyze, and draw conclusions from data. The two major areas of statistics are descriptive and inferential statistics. Statistics can be used to make better-informed business and investing decisions."

Supply Chain

According to Wikipedia: "In commerce, a supply chain is a system of organizations, people, activities, information, and resources involved in supplying a product or service to a consumer."

Survey

A survey or questionnaire, according to Qualtrics: "Fundamentally, a survey is a method of gathering information from a sample of people, traditionally with the intention of generalizing the results to a larger population. Surveys provide a critical source of data and insights for nearly everyone engaged in the information economy, from businesses and the media to government and academics."

Toolbox Trap

The "Toolbox-Trap", as defined by Diederik Martens, is when people and companies assume that implementing plus training technology by itself will result in success. Technology is not a magical button for success. According to Chaploop™, technology must also be levered with best-practices in Engagement, Talent, Data, and Integrations. People must focus on four pillars to increase the chance of success: Technology, Data, Process, and Change Management, according to Harvard Business Review.

Top-of-Funnel (TOFU)

According to TechTarget: "ToFu, MoFu and BoFu is a method used by sales and marketing professionals to pace and cater their approach to sales leads within a sales funnel, depending on the customer's current phase of the purchase decision. The stage names are abbreviations and refer to the sales funnel, which describes casting a wide net to attract leads, with a narrowing approach toward the bottom of the funnel, ending in sales. ToFu, MoFu and BoFu stand for top-of-funnel, middle-of-funnel and bottom-of-funnel, respectively."

Tracking

According to ChooseToEncrypt: "Generally, tracking involves collecting information about your use of or interaction with a particular web page. Web trackers can collect more information than just your browsing of a website. Websites also use them to collect your personal information: your IP address, where you came from, your geographic location and your browser characteristics. The websites that track you use three main methods: cookies, fingerprinting, and beacons. Websites may identify you with your login credentials, unique device identifiers or your IP-Address. Once a site determines your identity, it then assembles all the information it collects about you in a data profile.". *Also see 'Script', 'Cookie', 'IP-Address', 'and Website'.*

Transformation

According to CIO.com: "Digital transformation marks a radical rethinking of how an organization uses technology, people, and processes to fundamentally change business performance, says George Westerman, MIT principal research scientist and author of Leading Digital: Turning Technology into Business Transformation. Ideally led by the CEO, in partnership with CIOs, CHROs and other senior leaders, digital transformation requires cross-departmental collaboration in pairing business-focused philosophies with rapid application development models. Such sweeping changes are typically undertaken in pursuit of new business models and new revenue streams, driven by changes in customer expectations around products and services.". *Also see 'C-Level'.*

Ungated Content

Content that is openly available. There's no requirement to fill out a form. Opposite of 'Gated Content'. *Also see 'Content' and 'Form'.*

User Acceptance Test (UAT)

According to the ISTQB: "Formal testing with respect to user needs, requirements, and business processes conducted to determine whether a system satisfies the acceptance criteria and to enable the user, customers or other authorized entity to determine whether to accept the system."

User Group

According to Wikipedia: "A user group is a type of club focused on the use of a particular technology."

UTM-Tagging

According to Hubspot: "UTM codes are snippets of text added to the end of a URL to help you track where website traffic comes from if users click a link to this URL. Marketers can customize this text to match the webpage this URL is linked on, allowing them to attribute the success of that campaign to specific pieces of content."

Value Proposition

See 'proposition'

Vertical

According to Investopedia: "A vertical market is a market encompassing a group of companies and customers that are all interconnected around a specific niche. Companies in a vertical market are attuned to that market's specialized needs and generally do not serve a broader market. As such, vertical markets typically have their own set of business standards."

Viral

According to TycheSoftwares: "This is referred to as a media material like articles, images or videos that spread rapidly online through website links and social sharing channels. It is basically a kind of online content that appeals the users to share it or something that gets a lot of views, reads, clicks etc."

Webinar

According to G2: "A webcast or webinar (a combination of the words 'web' and 'seminar') is a video workshop, lecture, or presentation hosted online using webinar software. Often business-related, these sessions can be used to share knowledge, ideas, and updates with people around the world. Webinars can also be leveraged to build and nurture relationships, build authority around a brand, or demonstrate a product."

Whitepaper

According to Hubspot: "A whitepaper is a persuasive, authoritative, in-depth report on a specific topic that presents a problem and provides a solution."

What's In It For Them (WIIFT)

According to ThePowerMoves: "It postulates that if you want to influence people, you should highlight what they stand to gain in doing what you are proposing."

DISCLAIMER

This book is designed to provide information on working with marketing technology. It is sold with the understanding that the publisher and author are not engaged in rendering legal, accounting, or other professional services.

If legal or other expert assistance is required, the services of a competent professional should be sought. It is not the purpose of this book to reprint all the information that is otherwise available to marketing professionals and/or business leaders. But instead to complement, amplify, and supplement other texts.

You are urged to read all the available material, learn as much as possible about making marketing technology work, and tailor the information to your individual needs.

Marketing technology is not a magic solution to drive business value out of the box.

Anyone who decides to improve- and make their marketing technology work must expect to invest a lot of time and effort into it.

Every effort has been made to make this book as complete and as accurate as possible. However, there may be mistakes, both typographical and in content. Therefore, this text should be used only as a general guide and not as the ultimate source of making marketing technology work.

Furthermore this book contains information on marketing technology that is current only up to the printing date. The purpose of this book is to educate and entertain. The author shall have neither liability nor responsibility to any person or entity with respect to any loss or damage caused, or alleged to have been caused, directly or indirectly, by the information contained in this book.

If you do not wish to be bound by the above, you should try to return this book unused to the publisher for a full refund.

Printed in Poland
by Amazon Fulfillment
Poland Sp. z o.o., Wrocław

90480747R00128